Hope
FROM THE
Ashes

Hope
FROM THE
Ashes

INSIGHTS AND RESOURCES FOR WELCOMING LENTEN VISITORS

Paul E. Jarzembowski

FOREWORD BY
Most Reverend Frank J. Caggiano

Paulist Press
New York / Mahwah, NJ

Library of Congress Cataloging-in-Publication Data
Names: Jarzembowski, Paul E., author.
Title: Hope from the ashes : insights and resources for welcoming Lenten visitors / Paul E. Jarzembowski.
Description: New York /Mahwah, NJ : Paulist Press, [2022] | Summary: "This book explores the phenomenon that millions of people who are not regular churchgoers come back to receive ashes and engage in Lenten practices every year. It is packed with ideas for pastoral leaders to help their congregations accompany newcomers and visitors, many of them young adults, throughout Lent and beyond—turning moments of return into memorable milestones on their faith journey"—Provided by publisher.
Identifiers: LCCN 2021026653 (print) | LCCN 2021026654 (ebook) | ISBN 9780809155750 (paperback) | ISBN 9781587689741 (ebook)
Subjects: LCSH: Lent. | Ash Wednesday services. | Worship programs. | Public worship—Catholic Church. | Non-church-affiliated people. | Catholic Church—Customs and practices.
Classification: LCC BV85 .J37 2022 (print) | LCC BV85 (ebook) | DDC 252/.62—dc23
LC record available at https://lccn.loc.gov/2021026653
LC ebook record available at https://lccn.loc.gov/2021026654

ISBN 978-0-8091-5575-0 (paperback)
ISBN 978-1-58768-974-1 (e-book)

Published by Paulist Press
997 Macarthur Boulevard
Mahwah, New Jersey 07430
www.paulistpress.com

Printed and bound in the
United States of America

This book is dedicated to my mom and dad,
who first introduced me to and supported my lifelong
fascination and engagement with Lent;
to the late Fr. Richard Ameling,
my childhood pastor who inspired me
to service in the Church;
and to my wife, Sarah, whose
constant and loving companionship over the years
is a model of what true accompaniment
can and should always be.

CONTENTS

FOREWORD

Most Reverend Frank J. Caggiano

Bishop of the Roman Catholic Diocese of Bridgeport in Connecticut

They are memories that I will never forget, for they are all about ashes.

As a young boy, I still remember sitting in church, impressed by the large crowds of people who came on a Wednesday afternoon to quietly await their turn to receive a curious gift of ashes on their foreheads. I recall my mother drawing me closer to her as the number of people in the pew continued to swell. Despite the large number who patiently waited outside of our small wooden church, I can still remember the silence of that place. It was a silence that was unforgettable.

As people returned from their encounter with the priest, I recall seeing the ashen crosses that marked their foreheads, the ashes at times slowly falling away in the breeze that their movement created. After everyone received their curious gift, we left church to resume the rhythm of the day, all the while proclaiming to the world that we were dust and unto dust we would one day return.

Hope FROM THE Ashes

These vivid images from my youth remind me of the primordial power that ashes have to call us to silence, reflection, prayer, and witness. It was a time in my early faith formation that did not require words or lesson plans. It required only an encounter with ashes.

Ashes speak to the human heart, to believers and nonbelievers alike. They provoke questions that can be successfully delayed for a time but not avoided forever. For a Christian, they symbolize the entrance into the Lenten journey, inviting us to burn away our sins and all that hampers us from living a life of joy and freedom. Lent asks us to walk with the Lord into the ashen desert where he will teach us what must become ashes in our lives, so that we can rediscover that our spiritual ashes can lead to resurrected life that arises out of an empty tomb.

Among the tools of faith, there are few more powerful to touch human hearts than the power of ashes. It is a tool that has been long underestimated until now. The powerful insights offered in this book, *Hope from the Ashes*, provide us timely, practical, and pastoral ways by which we can engage people who remain drawn to the power of ashes. In light of the challenges we face both as the Church and as a society, this book is needed now more than ever.

In our age of never-ending activity and a growing inability to quiet our hearts to discover the peace for which we long, *Hope from the Ashes* gives us a roadmap by which we can intentionally engage those who remain drawn to the rituals of Ash Wednesday to walk their personal Lenten journey, accompanied by welcoming and loving communities of faith. For if we desire to engage those who have questions or doubts or have become indifferent to the practice of the faith, we can use the creative and practical advice in this book to walk with them in faith. We can help them to encounter a God who will take their spiritual ashes, often accumulated from their hurts, failures, and sins, and lead them to healing and peace in Christ. The reward for those who walk with such sisters and brothers is also to rediscover healing and new life for themselves.

Such an invitation is needed for people of all ages. It takes on greater urgency if we wish to invite young adults to walk their journeys of faith. Many times, they are genuinely searching for answers to the deepest questions of their lives. However, they often search for God without the support and accompaniment of a community of faith. Yet, as ashes speak deeply to their hearts, we have an opportunity to listen to their concerns, provide a genuine welcome, and accompany them to find answers to their questions. The pastoral suggestions offered in this book are of the greatest importance for anyone who desires to journey with people of all generations to discover the One who is speaking to their hearts.

For over fifty years, there have been many resources that address the work of the New Evangelization that began with Saint Paul VI. Yet I have rarely encountered any book that provides insights, advice, and challenges as timely and practical as those found in *Hope from the Ashes*. I invite you to read this book with an open heart, allowing its words to speak to your spirit as well as to your mind. For its true power lies beyond what our minds can reason on their own.

It lies in the power of ashes.

PREFACE

Just Your Typical Ash Wednesday

Your Father who sees what is hidden…
(Matt 6:18)

—from the Ash Wednesday Gospel Reading

Walking into church one Ash Wednesday evening a few years ago, it was hard to find a seat. This was not my normal Sunday experience. I struggled to find a decent place to sit in the church, like waiting in a crowded line for my favorite ride at Walt Disney World.

Thinking back, it went something like this: I managed to locate a spot in the middle of a pew near the back of the church. As I apologized to those already seated, I jostled my way past them to the midpoint of the pew. Looking around, I did not recognize the faces of the people I just passed. While I had come to this church regularly, the individuals I encountered were new to me. I smiled courteously and nodded to them but wondered, Who are these people and where are they coming from?

At that moment, I noticed that the back wall of the church was lined with people who were unable to find a seat or opted to stand rather than squeeze between strangers, as I had just done. There still was a constant stream of individuals pouring in from the parking lot. They, too, would have to stand shoulder to shoulder somewhere in this place, which seemed to be reaching its fire code capacity very quickly. Then someone announced from the front of the church, "Please move to the middle of the row, so those standing can find available seats." After all this commotion, the Mass finally began, a few minutes after the hour.

I turned my attention to the readings—the same ones as every year. On that Ash Wednesday, perhaps looking for a distraction from the fellow worshipers literally centimeters from me, I listened a bit more closely and heard them anew. The lector read from the book of the prophet Joel:

> Even now, says the LORD,
>   return to me with your whole heart,
>   with fasting, and weeping, and mourning;
>   Rend your hearts, not your garments,
>   and return to the LORD, your God.

As the words "return to me" passed the lector's lips, I could not help but think of the strangers on either side of me, and I reflected to myself, Are these men and women the ones who returned to church after being gone for a while? Is that why I did not recognize them? As those thoughts crowded my mind, I began to feel a bit guilty for silently judging them and getting frustrated with them for crowding me out of my favorite pew. After the cantor sang a wonderful psalm and we all responded, "Be merciful, O Lord, for we have sinned," another lector rose to her feet to proclaim a reading from Saint Paul's Second Letter to the Corinthians, and about halfway through, I heard these words:

Working together, then,
we appeal to you not to receive the grace of God
in vain. (2 Cor 6:1)

It occurred to me, as those words slipped into my consciousness, at that very uncomfortable and overcrowded moment, I
had discovered an opportunity for grace. As I looked around
the church and saw faces that I had never seen, I started to
recognize that this was really a blessing. Week after week, I
had bemoaned the fact that fewer and fewer people were
coming to church. And yet, on this one day, that trend was
inverted. Perhaps I had taken this grace of God in vain for so
many Ash Wednesdays before.

As those thoughts came over me, it was then time to
stand up for the Gospel reading. Awkwardly under such
crowded circumstances, we all rose to our feet and stretched
as the cantor sang a poignant verse: "If today you hear his
voice, harden not your hearts." O Lord, I prayed, may my own
heart not be hardened.

The Gospel proclaimed was a familiar one, from Saint
Matthew's account of the Sermon on the Mount, in which
Jesus taught us to pray, give alms, and fast—the three pillars
of Lenten observance. Ironically, in a space where we literally
watched each other pray, where we publicly passed a collection plate, and where we began our forty days of fasting with
the visible mark of ashes on our foreheads, Jesus was telling
us not to be like the hypocrites who pray, give, and fast in
such a visible manner; rather, he told us,

Do not let your left hand know what your right is
doing,...
go to your inner room,
close the door, and pray to your Father in
secret....

Hope FROM THE Ashes

Anoint your head and wash your face,
so that you may not appear to be fasting,
except to your Father who is hidden.
And your Father who sees what is hidden will
repay you. (Matt 6:3–6, 17–18)

The words "your Father who sees what is hidden" came over me in a new way that day. My perspective on most Ash Wednesdays had often been self-focused and myopic, but now I saw a "hidden" reality I had missed year after year. Many of those I called strangers, those who came less frequently to church, had much in their lives that was hidden to me. I really did not know their circumstances or reasons that may have kept them away or that drew them to church to receive ashes. While my civility was still intact as I benignly nodded and smiled to the people around me that day, my judgment of others still eclipsed any compassion or understanding I might have had for their realities. Yet the God "who sees what is hidden" knew, and if I sought to follow the will of the Lord in Lent or, for that matter, at any time of the year, I had to begin to see as the Father sees.

Since this realization washed over me that one Ash Wednesday, the moment has taken on new significance for me. Rather than being a day of mourning and sorrow, it has become a day of celebration like the shepherd who says, "Rejoice with me, for I have found my sheep that was lost" (Luke 15:6), the woman who says, "Rejoice with me, for I have found the coin that I had lost" (Luke 15:9), or the father who says, "We had to celebrate and rejoice, because this brother of yours was dead and has come to life; he was lost and has been found" (Luke 15:32).

The scene felt so familiar to me because I have had similar experiences nearly every single Ash Wednesday before that fateful day, no matter where I was. In fact, this is likely a typical Ash Wednesday in most Christian congregations across the United States.

I say Christian because this is something experienced not just by Roman Catholics like me. It is a story that many Lutherans, Methodists, Episcopalians, and Presbyterians, as well as a growing number of reformed and evangelical Christians, could tell on their Ash Wednesdays too. The desire for ashes is felt by those from almost all cultural families and ethnic groups. Ash Wednesday has also been a global moment of solidarity, in which large crowds gather in cathedrals, shrines, and country churches all around the world.

Each year, men and women continue to descend on churches and Christian communities for Ash Wednesday and, throughout the Lenten season, record numbers of people keep true to the promises they made on Lent's first day, culminating in increased engagement in Holy Week. However, in the weeks following Easter, crowds begin to disperse, attendance drops, and religious praxis falls by the wayside for many, at least until Ash Wednesday comes around again the following year.

Aside from Lent, the connection to the practice of faith has statistically fallen in recent years, especially among young adults in their twenties and thirties. Attendance at Mass and participation in the life of local faith communities and ministries have decreased. Meanwhile, people's pastoral needs have only increased: mental health, family struggles, economic uncertainties, fears, and anxieties, just to name a few. The anomaly of heightened Ash Wednesday engagement, then, is a phenomenon that can challenge us to look with fresh eyes and act with clean hearts. It is a call to action—to "harden not [our] hearts" (Ps 95:8), to work together and reach out with compassion to "what is hidden" (Matt 6:18): in other words, those who reconnect and those in need of pastoral accompaniment, seeking renewal and refuge in the arms of the Lord.

Hope FROM THE Ashes

Over the past twenty years, I have spent time listening to the stories of colleagues and friends from around the world about their Ash Wednesday and Lent experiences. So many of them had something insightful to share and their witness propelled me to write this book. I also wanted to use some of those insights to help tell this story for you, the reader. You will find these reflections scattered throughout the book. Some have given me permission to share their full names and others did not. This exercise in listening and reflecting on others' stories is itself a recommended best practice. No matter what I or these people say here, it is always good to take the time yourself to listen to those around you and prayerfully discover for yourself how best to move forward.

The insights and resources in this book can be a guide for anyone active in their faith—pastors, church staff and leadership, active members, and regular churchgoers with a heart for those who feel disconnected from faith or community. If you, too, have noticed large crowds of people receiving ashes or if you have spoken with someone who is unexpectedly keeping the Lenten fast, this book is for you. It is a missionary opportunity for everyone concerned about the present and future of faith communities. A simple act of welcoming a Lenten visitor can transform our chance encounters on Ash Wednesday from being brief moments of return into milestones of faith along our mutual journey toward the Lord.

ACKNOWLEDGMENTS

The journey of this book began many years ago when I noticed unusual trends in increased young adult engagement on Ash Wednesday. It grew along with my understanding of pastoral accompaniment, especially as seen in the pontificate of Pope Francis, who first deserves my gratitude for his profound leadership. It would be impossible to acknowledge all those who have shaped and molded my understanding, thinking, and writing. If someone is reading this book and recalls a conversation with me about Lent, please know that I am also incredibly grateful for your role throughout my personal development. You, too, have contributed to this book.

There are several people I wish to call out by name for their immediate connection to the production of this work. I begin by thanking my mom and dad, two of the people to whom this book is dedicated. As parents, they (along with my grandparents) introduced me to the traditions and experiences of Lent. I also credit them with showing me plenty of biblical epics, which fueled my imagination and an appreciation of the gospel story. They supported me as I developed my love of Lent and continue to be a beacon of encouragement today.

Other individuals who have formed, inspired, and supported me on this journey over the years include Fr. Richard Ameling; Fr. Patrick Brennan; Fr. Rafael Capó; Deacon Jerry

Christensen; Fr. John Cusick; Dr. Eileen Daily; Dr. timone davis; Fr. Frank Donio, SAC; Fr. Dave Dwyer, CSP; Fr. Greg Friedman, OFM; Gerard Gallagher; Dr. Peter Gilmour; Dr. Mark Grey; John and Nicole Perone Grosso; Vicky Hathaway; Rev. Heidi Haverkamp; Mike Hayes; Dr. Andrew Lichtenwalner; Dominic Lombardi; Ron Lovatt; Dr. Bob and Maggie McCarty; Barbara McCrabb; Katie Prejean McGrady; Bishop Dale Melczek; Fr. Andrew Menke; Mar Munoz-Visoso; Dr. Fred Niedner; Matt and Cassandra Palmer; Dr. James Papandrea; Dr. Bob Rice; Marilyn Santos; Archbishop J. Peter Sartain; Fr. Ed Shea, OFM; Marc and Paula Willard; Fr. Jim Wozniak; Frank Zolvinski; and the many who have accompanied me in my Lenten endeavors at Andrean High School, the Diocese of Gary, the Diocese of Joliet, Holy Family Parish (Inverness, IL), Saint Joseph and Saint Maria Goretti Parishes (Dyer, IN), Saint Theresa Parish (Palatine, IL), Valparaiso University, and my Sigma Tau Gamma fraternity brothers. I am also indebted to colleagues and others who offered invaluable insights through the survey I conducted while writing. While only some of their many thoughts were included in the book, all have been incredibly helpful to me.

I thank my office colleagues, and the episcopal leadership of the United States Conference of Catholic Bishops (USCCB), where I have had the honor to serve in ministerial leadership. The USCCB, along with my previous workplaces in Chicago and Joliet, have been wonderful places that have supported my passion for this topic and where I continued to grow, learn, and try to make a difference.

I wish to extend further gratitude to Amy S. McEntee, who directly helped me through the writing and editorial processes and whose professional collaboration and friendship I have treasured through the years; to Bishop Frank Caggiano, for his wonderful collegial support and mentorship through the years (and for graciously writing the foreword

Acknowledgments

to this book); and to my editor, Diane Vescovi, who, with the team at Paulist Press, helped me to shape and mold this manuscript into a finished product.

In a very special way, I express boundless gratitude to my loving wife, Sarah. She has patiently accompanied me as I imagined the concept for this book, listened and provided creative ideas during my brainstorming and writing, and whose own pastoral example, shown to me every day, became the inspiration for my work. I thank her for walking beside me on this journey and giving me the confidence I needed to transform an idea into a reality.

Finally, I offer my humble thanks to God. The Lord's Word in Scripture and in the depths of my prayer guided me every step of this pilgrim way. My favorite time to write was in the early morning hours and, as the sun rose each day I worked on the manuscript, I could see hope etched in the heavens by the Father. This is the same hope, rising out of the ashes of the darkness of night, that God offers to every pastoral leader and to every individual who has received ashes, no matter their religious engagement, all of whom remain in my heart as I share their stories with the readers of this book. May God be with us all.

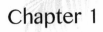

Chapter 1

THE LENTEN PHENOMENON

Even now, says the LORD, return to me.
(Joel 2:12)

—from the Ash Wednesday First Reading

Is the influx of people coming to church on Ash Wednesday just happening in my community or is this something bigger? How far does this phenomenon stretch?

The stories of many active churchgoers on Ash Wednesday are surprisingly similar. Each of us could probably recount our own stories of Ash Wednesdays past. After months of seeing the same faces in our pews, we often are greeted on the first day of Lent by faces unfamiliar to us. We probably are used to seeing a certain number of people inside our churches, but on this midwinter Wednesday, our churches, community centers, cathedrals, and parking lots are bursting with visitors. Perhaps we cannot find a good parking spot. Perhaps, upon entering, we find our favorite pew already occupied without room to spare, causing us to stand along a back wall. Or perhaps we look around the church and see

1

people we had not talked to in ages or individuals who we have never seen before this moment.

We could share similar stories, because these experiences are not limited to our local communities. The Ash Wednesday surge is a global and ecumenical phenomenon and has been for quite some time. Each year, without exception, most mainline Christian churches around the world are more crowded on Ash Wednesday than on any given Sunday. This is especially true for Roman Catholic and liturgical Protestant churches, but, in recent years, this trend has also extended to evangelical communities.

This phenomenon has become more noticeable and has taken on added significance in recent years, as weekly church attendance has dramatically declined and religious disaffiliation is on the rise, especially among young adults in their twenties and thirties. Gallup recently noted that only 47 percent of Americans now belong to a church, synagogue, mosque, or other religious community.[1] Recent studies of Christian worship practices found that church attendance among those in the two youngest adult generations today (known as millennials, born between 1980 and 1994, and Gen Z, born between 1995 and 2005) is at its lowest in recent memory. In fact, among Roman Catholics, only 14 percent of twenty- and thirty-somethings who self-identify with that religious expression come to church on a weekly basis.[2] This means that the other 85 percent are coming much less frequently, if at all.

While the number of active members and regular Sunday churchgoers has certainly diminished, the number of people receiving ashes on the first day of Lent still remains very high—and, in some instances, has even increased among the younger generations. In the Roman Catholic Church, while less than one in every four adults comes to church on a weekly basis, almost half attend Ash Wednesday services annually.[3]

The Lenten Phenomenon

Each year, local communities recognize this stunning phenomenon, scheduling additional church services to accommodate the anticipated number of attendees. My mother, who has served as office manager for her church in northwest Indiana for three decades, has firsthand experience of this. She told me, "Through all of this time, I have found that one of my busiest phone times is the week before Ash Wednesday. It seems everyone wants to have ashes on the forehead. This is even busier than Christmas or Easter!"[4] Church offices like hers are often flooded by phone calls and emails from people asking questions like "What time are ashes?" or "Will the ashes be given out before, during, or after the service?"

This phenomenon of increased participation is not limited to Ash Wednesday. The whole season of Lent is impacted. A Catholic research group at Georgetown University noted the following:

> Among Catholics who attend Mass at least once a month, those of the youngest generation, the Millennials, are the *most* likely to observe Lenten practices. More than nine in ten of these Catholics abstain from meat on Fridays (91 percent) and receive ashes on Ash Wednesday (91 percent). About three-quarters of these young Mass-attending Catholics (74 percent) also give up something during Lent (besides meat on Fridays). A similar percentage (75 percent) make other extra positive efforts.[5]

Among Christians who join a church or attend worship services even less frequently, Ash Wednesday and Lenten customs are still incredibly popular. One in four will still attempt to do something positive for the forty days following Ash Wednesday, and over 40 percent of those same individuals abstain from eating meat during the Fridays of Lent.[6] Given the sobering trends experienced by many churches today, Ash Wednesday and Lent truly stand out as occasions of connection.

A MOMENT LIKE NO OTHER

This increase in religious practice is notable in part because, aside from Mardi Gras, nothing prior to Ash Wednesday prepares and promotes this season in the collective consciousness. There are no preparatory calendars (like in Advent), no holiday shopping season, and no movies or television specials to serve as a constant reminder of the forthcoming religious observance, as for Christmas and Easter. Homes are not decorated for Lent, and family dinners are not typically planned to celebrate Ash Wednesday; there are no parades, gifts, greeting cards. Still, despite the lack of attention in popular and religious culture, something about these Lenten moments of faith attracts people year after year after year.

Take, for example, Saint Peter's in the Loop, a Catholic church in the heart of the business district in downtown Chicago. Each Ash Wednesday, at least twelve Masses are celebrated in the upper church, while the imposition of ashes takes place continuously for thirteen consecutive hours in the lower-level auditorium. Additionally, the sacrament of reconciliation is offered for twelve or more hours in the confessionals on either side of the church. Almost every liturgy is packed, confessions are heard continuously, and, for most of the day, a line of people waiting to receive ashes stretches for several blocks.

Most of these people crowded into Saint Peter's are not regular parishioners. Many are young adults in their twenties and thirties. Most are young professionals who live in the Chicago neighborhoods or the surrounding suburbs and work Monday through Friday in the office buildings nearby.

Other visitors include Chicago police and municipal employees, students at the city colleges and universities around the Loop, cashiers, baristas, and stock room clerks who manage the nearby shopping and entertainment districts, construction workers, engineers, city planners, and sightseeing tourists from out of town. Some who stand in line to receive ashes have no faith community of their own, and a few may not have practiced their faith in decades.

On Ash Wednesday, however, they all stand together in anticipation of receiving ashes and taking a few moments for quiet prayer. The same scene can be found in many urban settings (Saint Patrick's Cathedral in New York, for example), and the experiences are similar in almost every mainline Christian church in the suburbs, small towns, and rural communities across North America (and in many other parts of the world), not to mention train platforms and parking lots; community centers, nursing homes, and prisons; military base chapels and college campuses. On Ash Wednesday, a massive influx of men, women, and children make their way to these places simply to receive a sprinkle of ash upon their forehead. This singular and special moment is a phenomenon like none other.

MOMENTS OF RETURN

While the tradition of Lent stretches back to the earliest days of Christian history, this worldwide *moment* of return is a relatively new phenomenon. In previous generations, after a disruption in active religious engagement—going off to college or leaving the family home—people eventually would make a more permanent return to their faith community. Single young people would often return to religious practice when they got married or, if not then, when they started having children. When a person returned, it was for a lifetime.

However, fewer people are engaging in these once-typical long-lasting return experiences associated with marriage or the birth of a child. Rather, people are returning for brief encounters: perhaps for an hour, or to attend a wedding, funeral, or Christmas celebration, however long they might last.

Today, the most noticed moments of return are Christmas and Easter, considered by many as the two holiest days of the Christian year. On these two holidays, which also have been widely secularized, those who return often are accompanied by family (parents, grandparents, siblings, or children) to celebrate these popular religious occasions.

Other moments include the wedding ceremonies of friends or family members (who may or may not be active churchgoers themselves), the baptisms of friends' or family members' children, or the funeral services of loved ones. Like Christmas and Easter, what marks almost all of these occasions are that these chance visits rarely are done alone; rather, they are experienced in the company of familiar faces. Since a great number of these events occur outside a normal weekend church service, there is little interaction with a regular churchgoing community, except for a priest, deacon, or some lay staff person who organizes these activities.

Moments are by definition brief, temporary, and fleeting. They will, and often do, come and go without much proactive effort on the part of the church or community that experiences the company of visitors and newcomers for these moments of return. We often forget these moments soon after they occur, as we return to our spiritual routine.

Perhaps it is fitting that the first words of the first reading we all hear on Ash Wednesday are "Yet even now, says the LORD, return to me with all your heart" (Joel 2:12). There is something about "yet even now" that has brought people to reconnect for this moment in time. It is as if God is asking us to stop from our routines and examine the here and "now."

Wouldn't it be wonderful, then, to turn these *moments* into *milestones*? Wouldn't it be great if people felt as comfortable coming to church on any given Sunday as they do during the moments of return? Wouldn't it be spectacular if Ash Wednesday were just the first day, the first milestone of a person's renewed spiritual journey, feeling that they really belong to a loving and supportive community of Christians?

When we offer more intentional accompaniment at a moment of return, we can help people feel that they belong— they are appreciated, understood, supported, valued, loved, and more connected to God. The Ash Wednesday phenomenon can lead us to *What if?* scenarios to act upon.

- *What if* people on Ash Wednesday felt they truly belonged to the community that welcomes them?
- *What if* those who return to church on Ash Wednesday knew that whatever comprises their life story thus far, they are loved and accepted for who God made them to be?
- *What if* an individual who walked into church alone on Ash Wednesday left feeling they had a connection to at least two other people at the end of that first day of Lent?
- *What if* someone who fasts every Friday during Lent began to come to church every Sunday after Lent?
- *What if* a person's experience of fasting for forty days was just the first step on their journey of faith engagement that lasted a lifetime?

If we acknowledge this phenomenon and use this God-given opportunity to genuinely accompany those who reconnect with religious practice during Lent each year, it is very possible there will be increased participation and engagement in our churches and communities, perhaps most visible among the young adult population. Should we develop a warm, welcoming, and hospitable spirit in the season of Lent, members of local communities might also become more bonded to one another. Possibly parishes might once more become *family*, where nearly everyone is concerned for and cares for each other—and no one would be left behind. By transforming our Christian communities into places of refuge on Ash Wednesday, or on any day in the season of Lent, our churches can become truly safe spaces and oases of peace and calm in a world in turmoil. If we make this corporate Lenten resolution as a community—to welcome the lost and accompany the stranger—and embrace those goals any time of year, our churches can truly follow in the footsteps of the Good Shepherd who gathers his sheep together.

THE HISTORIC RESILIENCY OF ASH WEDNESDAY

The power of the ashes is nothing new. Ash Wednesday has been somewhat of a phenomenon for ages. In tenth-century England, an abbot by the name of Ælfric delivered a memorable Ash Wednesday homily in which he connected the congregation's reception of ashes to an ancient custom of covering oneself with ashes and sitting in sackcloth. Then he made an interesting aside—or what may be a dire warning. He recounted the story of a man who refused to go to church on Ash Wednesday and was brutally killed a few days later by being attacked by hounds and impaled by his own spear![7] For the medieval abbot, sacramental ashes held an incredible power, so much so that to miss the chance might lead to a horrible fate. The possibility of being mauled by a pack of hounds may not compel people today to receive ashes, but it does speak to the powerful draw this experience has had for centuries.

As Ælfric noted, the basis of Ash Wednesday originates long before the time of Jesus. Since ancient days, when the precursors of the Jewish people were a nomadic tribe in the deserts of the Middle East, people would cover themselves with sackcloth and ashes as a sign of mourning, penance, or punishment. Some scholars trace this custom as far back as ancient Babylon, when sackcloth was worn by those who buried the dead while they sprinkled ash on the forehead and on the graves of the deceased during funeral rites.[8] In these nascent societies, where pain and death were viewed as divine punishment, the physical discomfort of goat's hair coarsely grating against the skin and the black soot from the desert floor baking a person in the midday sun were ways to publicly manifest one's grief.

There are many instances of this practice in Scripture: the patriarch Jacob put sackcloth on his loins when he heard of the supposed death of his son Joseph (see Gen 37:34); Job wore sackcloth and covered himself in ashes to mark his lament and suffering (see Job 16:15) and again to signal the conclusion of his mourning (see Job 42:6); the people of ancient Assyria put aside their pagan ways and "the king of Nineveh...rose from his throne, removed his robe, covered himself with sackcloth, and sat in ashes" (Jonah 3:6); and Jesus mentioned the ritual in his admonition of unrepentant villages saying, "Woe to you, Chorazin! Woe to you, Bethsaida! For if the deeds of power done in you had been done in Tyre and Sidon, they would have repented long ago in sackcloth and ashes" (Matt 11:21).

Furthermore, the power and resiliency of this practice was not limited to Near Eastern cultures. The ritual of sitting in sackcloth and ashes was used in parts of Europe as well. The Greek poet Homer noted in the eighth century BC that the great warrior Achilles, upon hearing of the death of his close friend Patroclus during the Trojan War, "cast on the ground, with furious hands he spread the scorching ashes o'er his graceful head" and then tore his fine garments, rolling and groveling in the dust.[9]

Because of its ubiquitous nature, the poignant custom of sitting in sackcloth and ashes remained the norm for individuals going through mourning, penance, and punishment in the various cultures that comprised the Roman Empire. While this practice most certainly was done in Jewish and Christian communities throughout the first and second centuries, we have historical records of sackcloth and ashes becoming an established part of Christian ritual by the third century. These earthen elements were components of an *order of penitents*, a rite that reunited with the Church already-baptized individuals who had committed serious sins.[10] The second-century North African Christian author Tertullian spoke of the discipline of separating a sinner from the rest of a congregation by instructing that person "to lie in sackcloth and ashes, to cover his body with filthy rags...[to] nourish prayer by fasting."[11]

As Easter became the most important day of remembrance for the early Christians, the need for a fast in preparation also developed. What we now know as Lent emerged slowly in those first centuries, with different intensities in the various corners of the Mediterranean world: to prepare the active Christian community for Easter; to provide time for the penance of sinners (including the *lapsi*, or lapsed Christians who denied their faith to avoid persecution); or to finalize the preparations for receiving catechumens or newcomers into the Church.[12] The historical records from the first Council of Nicaea indicate that the concept of Lent, if not its exact timing and length, was an established norm on the Christian liturgical calendar by the year 325.[13] The earliest Gregorian Sacramentary books, dated to the seventh or eighth centuries, are the first to mention *dies cinerum* (or "day of ashes").[14] In varied and often locally developed ways, the elements and experiences of what was to become Ash Wednesday and the rest of Lent evolved in fits and starts all across Europe, North Africa, and the Near East. The first true *worldwide* application of Ash Wednesday took place in the year 1091, when the Synod of Beneventum declared that every Christian ought to begin their Lent with a reception of ashes.[15] From then until now, Lent's resiliency has grown ever stronger, and its power globally resilient.

Today's active engagement in a forty-day fast is also deeply rooted in the Judeo-Christian tradition. From the beginning of the Christian experience, it was critical to connect one's Lenten praxis to the number forty, as it mirrored or echoed the great biblical experiences. Forty was the number of years the Israelites spent wandering in the desert before entering the promised land (see Exod 16:35); forty also marked the number of days that Moses spent on Mount Sinai to receive the Ten Commandments (cf. Exod 34:28), the days that Elijah traveled without food, fleeing from Jezebel after killing her pagan prophets (see 1 Kgs 19:7–8), and the period when Nineveh fasted and prayed after their citywide conversion (see Jonah 3:4). Most important for Christians, forty days was the timeframe that Jesus traversed the wilderness being tempted by the devil (cf. Matt 4:2; Mark 1:13; Luke 4:2). Through its development, Lent often reflected the darkness of medieval life, when the threat of death seemed imminent across a bleak, hostile environment. The season focused exclusively on self-denial and mortality, including the reminder of our fragile existence reflected in a biblical passage that accompanied the distribution of ashes: "You are dust and to dust you shall return" from Genesis 3:19. The notion of Lenten fasting, a tradition that has also existed since humanity's earliest days, was varied: no meat or other indulgences every day leading up to Easter, or every day except weekends, or except Sundays; no milk or eggs; just one small meal per day; or fasting on Wednesdays or Fridays or on both days.

Over time, this mortification had a backlash, as laypeople developed extravagant pre-Lenten customs of devouring their supply of meats and sweets in the weeks prior to the first day of Lent. These purging acts soon evolved into unbridled fits of revelry and celebration, which evolved into what we now know as Mardi Gras or Carnival (from the Latin *caro levare*, roughly translated as "to remove meat," and during the Middle Ages, as *carne vale*, or "farewell meat").[16]

One could argue that the popular rise of Carnival season solidified the resiliency and power of Ash Wednesday even further in public consciousness. The final day of the festivities became a liminal moment that separated two opposing experiences: gluttony and denial. It marked the barrier between celebration and introspection, indulgence and fasting, and merriment and mourning. The Mardi-Gras-to-Ash-Wednesday transition served as a critical inflection point. One could even argue that the combination of these two seemingly opposing holidays fueled their respective growth since the Renaissance. Over the past few centuries, Ash Wednesday and Lent continued to be widespread markers of popular piety, despite the tumult of potential resistance, including wars, plagues, reformations, and industrial and scientific revolutions.

Even the most recent global pandemic in 2020 and 2021, which shook the world's population, could not stop people from receiving ashes. During and just prior to the many shutdowns around the world and across their country, almost half

12

of all Roman Catholics in the United States attended Ash Wednesday services in person, making it the most-attended Church holiday of 2020.[17] In 2021, with most public celebrations being held with limited capacity, around fourteen million Roman Catholics still received ashes,[18] as millions more marked the day by participating via online services, with the distribution of ashes adapted to provide maximum health precautions.[19] Still, these changes and the availability of virtual celebrations did not prevent a significant number of people from receiving ashes in person at a church, despite the risks.

One can say that the observed phenomenon of atypical-sized crowds attending religious services on Ash Wednesday over the past several decades has been amplified due to today's historic disaffiliation that houses of worship have been facing. In a way, the anomaly of increased participation once per year, even in the face of a worldwide pandemic in recent years, runs counter to the experiences of other institutions, both secular and religious, which do not annually receive a moment of return like Christian churches do each Lent. This once again speaks to the sheer power of the phenomenon and the history still in the making to this very day.

ECUMENICAL AND GLOBAL SOLIDARITY

One example of the ecumenical power of Ash Wednesday came in the heart of the Reformation in Tudor England. When Henry VIII split from the Catholic Church in the early sixteenth century, reformers preached against the use of candles, palms, ashes, and other Roman elements in Christian worship. As one scholar noted, "The once prolific sacramentals, among them the characteristic Lenten ashes, were now under heavy repression."[20] Amid violent rebellions against the developing *Book of Common Prayer* in 1549, commoners rose up against the suppression and insisted, "We will have holy bread and holy water made every Sunday, palms and ashes at the times appointed and accustomed, images to be set up again in every church, and all other ancient old ceremonies used heretofore by our mother the holy Church."[21] As the Reformation unfolded and Protestants moved away from the practices of Roman Catholicism, the custom of ashes still remained as a constant in many emerging liturgical communities.

Ash Wednesday and Lent, we must remember, are beloved across Christian boundaries, not just among Catholics. Ashes and fasting are foundational elements to our shared Judeo-Christian roots, as this ritual has had a profound impact for many over the centuries as they harken back to a common and shared heritage. Perhaps most important, though, the ashes serve as a reminder of human brokenness and fragility ("Remember you are dust and to dust you shall return"), as well as resolution and renewal ("Repent [or turn away from sin] and be faithful to the Gospel"), which nearly every person of every Christian creed can affirm. To some extent, Ash Wednesday serves as a great bond that unites Christians for a moment, fulfilling Jesus's prayer in the Garden of Gethsemane when he said, "So that they may be one, as we are one" (John 17:22).

On Ash Wednesday, it is important to realize that the ashes on a person's forehead can belong to anyone—and not just those of our own denomination or community. Roman Catholics, Lutherans, Episcopalians, Methodists, Presbyterians, and members of several Reformed Churches all honor this day. When the ecumenical movement took root among Christians in the mid-twentieth century, many congregations looked to their origins and began to revive worship traditions that may have been disregarded in earlier centuries. For instance, the United Methodist Church noted that "the liturgical and theological restoration of this season has been a prime factor in the recovery of what is basic to the worship of Christian people everywhere."[22] One of these historical liturgical elements that returned was the use of ashes.

As an active member of his Reformed Christian community in northern Illinois, John—who did not grow up with any formal Lenten traditions—shared that his church has added five services on Ash Wednesday over the past decade: "We got a large influx of attendees who were previously Catholic and one of our pastors started it. It was well-received and has become a tradition....I have to admit that when I attend the service, doing something tangible like having ashes put on my forehead does somehow bring me into a different relationship to God."[23] Even Southern Baptist and other nonliturgical churches distribute ashes on occasion and offer special programming during Lent.

"In recent years, Christians from the Reformed branch of the Protestant tradition have begun to recover a practice... to begin Lent on the Wednesday before the first Sunday of Lent with a service of repentance and commitment, including the imposition of ashes," notes Christian author Blair Gilmer Meeks. She goes on to say, "The Lutheran and Anglican traditions, of course, never lapsed in this observance," and the "Ash Wednesday prayers of ancient origin found in denominational worship books bring us together ecumenically."[24] Because Christians engaged in the practices and traditions of Lent long before Christianity began to splinter, it is a common heritage for anyone who professes belief in Jesus Christ. For instance, to avoid seeming too ritualistic or liturgical, some Protestant churches, especially in evangelical and reformed communities, will host Ash Wednesday gatherings without the rite or imposition of ashes. It varies from location to location.

Episcopal priest and author Reverend Heidi Haverkamp shares that "everyone loves the spiritual wonder and joy at Advent, but it's so busy....Lent is a time where I see Christians of all denominations turn more seriously to their spiritual growth and worship." She personally loves the seriousness of the season because "nowhere else in our consumer society do people show up to be reminded that sin is real, that they are forgiven, but also that they're going to die—much less get a smudge of ash rubbed on their foreheads."[25]

Echoing this sentiment, Peggy Marks, a retired Lutheran pastor in New Jersey, notes that "Lent is such an important part of our year and an important process within our tradition....It moves us back to our roots." In her experience, many Lutherans look at the Lenten season "with less emphasis on giving up and more emphasis on taking something on...by giving more generously, by reading their Bible more often, or by doing more good in the world, wherever they can." She notes that there are indeed larger crowds who come on Ash Wednesday within the Lutheran communities at which she has served.[26]

Although denominational differences exist, this season offers common bonds and shared experiences, which have the incredible potential to bring people together. University and college campuses are great examples of places where active ecumenism exists in Lent, as several local churches or campus ministry groups from different Christian traditions will work together to host Ash Wednesday worship or engage in a service project or fasting to combat world hunger.

Because of the growing trend of religious disaffiliation in North America, coupled with an innate sense of spirituality within the population, the phenomena of reconnecting with faith traditions in Lent are indeed more noticeable in countries like the United States or Canada. In predominantly Christian countries such as Italy, Poland, or the Philippines, there is little *observable* change in people's participation on Ash Wednesday or with those more engaged in Lenten practices compared to the already-significant attendance at church every Sunday of the year. Nonetheless, massive participation on Ash Wednesday is still a global reality. One Polish journalist notes that "despite the fact the Wednesday [when] Lent begins is a workday, Poles still tend to go to church en masse on Popielec (Ash Wednesday) and take part in the rite."[27]

In Uganda in east-central Africa, "the situation varies from one province to another," according to Joyce Zako, staff to the Uganda Catholic Bishops Conference. "In some dioceses, there are tendencies of increased numbers of people during Ash Wednesday than the 'normal' Sunday Masses.... But in the rural areas, the number of the Christian population in each rural parish is almost constant." Joyce notes that the nature of a person's work or the businesses they undertake could determine how these trends play out. She notes that, though there are no local studies on this, it seems the majority of those who regularly engage with Lent are middle-aged adult women. Other populations, such as young people and adult males, may be in the group that reconnects with faith on occasion or only at Christmas, Easter, and Ash Wednesday.[28]

In Ireland, where a historically and intensely religious populace has become very secularized over the past few decades and church attendance has dropped precipitously, the reception of ashes becomes quite momentary and quick. Gerard Gallagher, an author and pastoral leader from the Catholic Diocese of Dublin, notes, "There are many stories of how many people came to attend Ash Wednesday—but just for the ashes. For some, the ashes form part of a popular piety that has no real connection to faith. I know of those who just want to get the ashes and not attend the Mass."[29] Record numbers of individuals who take part in the *drive-thru ashes* option in churches around Ireland testify to this trend.[30] Gerard has also noticed that young people who do remain actively connected to Catholic communities are beginning to privatize their spiritual practices, including Lenten fasting or other observances, to avoid ridicule in a country that is increasingly suspicious of religious institutions and wary of any hypocrisy on the part of religious adherents.[31]

. Fasting "makes sense" to most Germans—whether Lutheran, Catholic, or agnostic—according to pre-Lenten research done annually by the secular German health insurance company DAK.[32] Alcohol and sweets vie for the first place among fasting trends, followed by meats, television, and smoking. In recent years, however, the study found more Germans wanting to detach from their mobile devices and computers for Lent. An even more compelling fact about these studies is that young adults between thirty and forty-four years are most drawn to fasting and that those between nineteen and twenty-six are highly likely to restrict their use of technology.[33] In 2018, a group of northern German Lutheran communities partnered with a Roman Catholic diocese in lower Saxony for a "climate fast" that Lent, raising awareness of the faith dimension to ecological issues by using less energy and living more simply for the forty-day season.[34]

With its historical resiliency, ecumenical solidarity, and international scope, Lent is indeed a powerful moment in the life of faith. The draw or attraction to ashes and Lenten customs have withstood the test of time and the challenges of wars and pandemics and, still today, occupy a place of honor, even among those who are no longer that religious. Whereas in past generations, they may have been burdensome requirements, the spiritual themes and practices of the Lenten season often provide quiet, peace, and familiarity amid a chaotic world and moments of comfort and solace for people who struggle in today's challenging times.

"Yet even now" begins the first reading of Ash Wednesday from the prophet Joel. These three words have many meanings, but perhaps it is best to think of them in light of the long history and wide scope of this season and put them in conversation with the present age. One often hears the catastrophizing of the current moment—this is the worst time ever or it has never been this bad—about what a person is enduring here and now. Perhaps there is some truth to it, but these first words from Joel remind us of the sheer power of these moments of return in relation to the present circumstance, challenging us to explore this phenomenon of Ash Wednesday engagement more deeply and, "yet even now," respond as Christ would.

Chapter 2

STEPPING UP TO THE CHALLENGE

Then the LORD was stirred to concern.
(Joel 2:18)

—from the Ash Wednesday First Reading

Why do people come to church in droves on Ash Wednesday, fast on Fridays, or give up something for forty days? There is no single answer, but everyone has a story to tell.

Several years ago, Busted Halo, a Catholic digital outreach ministry to young adults in their twenties and thirties, interviewed people entering Saint Paul's Church in New York City on Ash Wednesday. The interviewers were curious why so many people were coming for ashes that day. Here are some of the responses:

- "I'm ready to repent and to spend the next few days thinking about ways to be a better Catholic and a better person in general."
- "I feel at peace. It'll probably make me feel better for the rest of the day."

- "It's almost like a tradition. My grandmother always made me do it."
- "The need for…divine blessing. To experience the relevance of God."
- "I went to Catholic school, so I've always known to go every Ash Wednesday."
- "To make a Lenten promise or commit to church….It's kind of a fresh start."[1]

Even in this small group of people, the answers were all over the board. What is remarkable is that Ash Wednesday—for Catholics—is not a holy day of obligation. It is not a solemnity or a significant feast day for a popular saint. It is simply the first day of a liturgical season. There is no canonical requirement that Catholics receive ashes or even attend Mass on Ash Wednesday. Yet, no matter how the Church views this occasion, the crowds seem to treat this day with an attention otherwise reserved for Christmas or Easter.

A young woman named Heather from Roslyn, Pennsylvania, shared with me that she does not attend church that much anymore, but she still comes to Mass each Ash Wednesday, noting with a certain frankness, "Honestly, for me there are certain days that feel 'special,' and I tend to feel more of an obligation to attend."[2] She is not alone in that compulsion. I suspect that many others who reconnect on Ash Wednesday are not thinking deeply about its history or meaning. They just come. Even if every church authority around the world deemed Ash Wednesday an official *holy day of obligation*, little would likely change. Everyone has their own reason and their own story. Many come because of something rooted within those stories. So, for us to respond effectively, it is crucial that we reflect on those reasons.

Let me first share a disclaimer before proceeding: Many assume too often that people receive ashes out of Catholic guilt, Christian obligation, or holy piety. Perhaps these reasons were predominantly true for previous generations when the strict observance of Lent was ingrained within the Christian cultural experience. Today, however, this is simply not the case. The growing disaffiliation from religious worship and church membership seems to indicate that fewer individuals are drawn in by guilt. Young adults, for instance, who grew up in the 1990s or 2000s (or later) did not experience the religious prescriptions of their parents or grandparents. And yet, their participation in Lenten practices is just as strong or stronger than their elders.

To truly understand the *why* behind it all, it is best to simply ask. Each person sitting in the pews on Ash Wednesday and everyone who gives up something for Lent has a unique story that led them to engage in those actions. While we know and can speak to our *own* experiences, we do not truly know that of *others*. It is critical to remember this point when thinking about those who reconnect. We must not presume or assume anything about them, project ourselves into their stories, or prejudge their rationale for reconnecting. Rather, we should ask about their journeys and listen. Even if they cannot articulate exactly what motivated them to walk into church, they still have a backstory to tell, and we have a responsibility to listen.

What follows are seven common threads I pieced together from the stories of people who have received ashes and partaken in Lenten traditions. That leads me to my second disclaimer: These are not the only reasons, and there will be nuances to these seven threads. It is not a scientific data collection but prayerful reflections and ruminations after listening carefully, observing this phenomenon firsthand, and doing my best (sometimes succeeding, sometimes failing) to accompany others along our respective paths. With that in mind, I offer these seven as starting points for church leaders to consider and reflect on as they approach and prepare for Lent in a more intentional and missionary way.

1. PEACE, REST, AND REFUGE

Our life stories often involve a combination of factors including mental and physical health concerns, economic uncertainty, marginalization, and varying degrees of stress. Technology and social communications, intended to make life easier, have added further layers of complications to our already-fractured lives. For many, the world is noisy, busy, and overwhelming. In response, many crave peace, rest, and refuge. For young adults especially, but increasingly for those of any generation, there are additional burdens of carving out a place in the world, discovering identity and purpose, and building up key relationships—all of which can quickly fall out of place. The COVID-19 global pandemic caused the work-life balance to blend, sometimes in unhealthy directions, with ramifications likely for decades to come. With wages remaining low and costs exponentially rising, many take multiple jobs, attempting to pay their bills and pull themselves out of debt. In the wake of this, domestic life, whether single, dating, or married, may break down, further adding to the existing stressors in one's life. Even for those who have a secure job, higher education, and access to health care, struggles still exist.

Faced with these challenges, sleep and rest often are neglected in favor of a job and other responsibilities. Many, especially young people, are just trying every day to dig themselves out from under the layers of stress and anxiety piled upon them. The world is steeped in pressure, insecurity, and pain. Perhaps this, more than anything else, is what contributes to the growing disaffiliation from religious practice.

Churches and other houses of worship, in large part, wrestle with how to respond in relevant ways to the crises people experience. Consequently, many who seek relief from the stress of the world may not look for it or find it in faith communities.

Each year, despite this mounting stress, many of those same exhausted and overwhelmed people come to church for one moment of peace and calm on Ash Wednesday or during Lent. Many are grateful for the simplicity of the structure that churches provide. They enjoy a lack of complications, ornamentation, and activity, basking in the quiet of a sanctuary as the church doors close out the noise of the world. With lives overflowing with constant stress and anxiety, the notion of emptiness and release can be a welcome experience many do not normally have. Tim from Valparaiso, Indiana, for instance, feels that Ash Wednesday is a "paradoxically beautiful reminder that there is more to life than this earth...even when things are bad."[3]

Additionally, the regularity and familiarity of Lenten rituals offer people an antidote to the perception that every day seems crazy and unpredictable. Being able to follow and flow through simple directives, some of which they have engaged in since childhood, can offer much-needed comfort for the frazzled person in the pews. The experiences of Ash Wednesday and Lent do not change much from year to year. The stable and familiar rituals are quite a blessing to the otherwise overwhelmed individual. Author, spiritual director, and retreat facilitator Becky Eldredge of Baton Rouge observes, "I think most Christians understand the value of what Jesus went through on our behalf. The structure and discipline of a set period of time to go deeper is comforting to people."[4] In the church, some might also discover a sense of Lenten peace and safety rather than the constant division and violent rhetoric they experience in everyday life. In the relative quiet of a church they can capture a bit of calm amid the chaos, silence amid the noise, and rest amid the restlessness. As we look around on Ash Wednesday, we are often unaware of the stories of frustration or angst that are stirring within the souls of the people we do not know. Yet for one moment, they have brought these feelings and emotions into our sacred space, laying them at the Lord's feet as they usually do around this time each passing year.

2. ACCESSIBLE SPIRITUALITY

Although increasing numbers of people are not attending church services on a regular basis, many individuals still feel *spiritual* through prayer and an affirmation of belief in a higher power. Evangelical pastor Dan Kimball says that these are good-hearted individuals "who like Jesus but not the church."[5] Many have noted those who identify as being *spiritual but not religious*—that is, those who avoid participating in the worship services of religious institutions but still find themselves in awe of a divine being or connect with Jesus who guides their lives. They pray privately, perhaps read their Bible on occasion, treat others fairly and kindly, do good works, celebrate Christmas, and, on occasion, do something religious.

Lent is a time when some of those who are spiritual but not religious reengage in Christian praxis and spirituality. On Ash Wednesday, people can slip into the back of a church and blend into the crowds. Lenten traditions like fasting and abstinence can be done at home, away from the possibility of being judged in public. Individuals can fast in a way that works best for them and to feel more connected to God, without the intervention of others. People can be mindful to avoid meat each Friday throughout Lent and, should they slip up one week, not feel they will be condemned.

During Lent, the Church also emphasizes the human-ity of Jesus. Consider that, throughout the Lenten season, we follow Jesus in the dramatic moments of his story: the har-rowing journey through the wilderness, the transfiguration on the mountaintop, the raising of Lazarus from the dead, and a triumphant entrance into Jerusalem, all culminating in the intensity of the Lord's final days on earth. Allison, a young adult from Palatine, Illinois, notices that, when Lent arrives, it is a special time "we walk with Jesus as he prepares for the cross,"[6] and Jennifer, from the nation of Malta, notes that Ash Wednesday is an annual opportunity to "reflect on how during the days of Lent I can strengthen my relationship with Jesus."[7]

Lent allows for an accessible spirituality where anyone can partake. One does not need to be a practicing Christian to receive ashes—just to make a humble admission of one's own mortality and a promise to sin no more and be faith-ful to God. At other times of year, a person might not feel they fit into a Christian community, perhaps because they perceive judgment for their wrongdoings or because they assume a level of religious competence or benchmarks. But on Ash Wednesday, one needs only to willingly admit their frailty and try their best to be a better person. This is acces-sible spirituality at its finest, allowing individuals to incorpo-rate religious praxis into their spiritual lives at their own pace over the course of the forty-day season.

3. MODERATE OR MODEST COMMITMENT

With increasingly busy and complicated lives, adults today do not have much time to spare. They are overwhelmed with jobs, family obligations, and building an identity in a chaotic world, and many are not able to stretch themselves any further. This heaviness also leads to the need for quick, easy answers. People are looking for spiritual practices that will fit into their busy lives. This can become habitual, and what we expect of our mobile devices can bleed into other parts of life too. The concept of instant spiritual gratification can be appealing. Lent, then, becomes an ideal experience for our current age: it is short, lasting about forty days; tangible, such as ashes on the forehead to express spiritual commitment; and has only three basic, easy-to-grasp commitments: to pray, fast, and give. Chris, a young adult consultant for the Catholic Church in Great Britain, observes, "It struck me that the tangible and visible symbol of the cross on the forehead was something that held great meaning for people. It's strange to say, but it felt like its symbolic value was greater than that of the regularly offered sacraments."[8]

Multiweek challenges, such as for weight loss and exercise, charitable or political causes, and personal growth, are also increasingly popular on social media. The idea of Lent, which has incorporated these elements for centuries, makes perfect sense for a postmodern mindset. Knowing that the commitment to buckle down lasts only forty days makes this exercise doable for anyone. And unlike a contract to a health club or a wireless plan, one does not need to formally commit to anything to engage in Lent.

Through Scripture and traditions of the season, Lent offers people the image of Christ in the fullness of his humanity, as he experiences temptations in the desert, breaks down in tears before Lazarus's tomb, and offers blood, sweat, and tears in prayer in the Garden of Gethsemane. It seems to mirror our own humanity, allowing us to feel we have permission to be comfortable in our own skin as we strive for holiness. Lent allows us to engage with spirituality or religiosity to the degree in which we are able. Lent reminds us that we are all human and may be able commit to only so much—and that's okay.

For those with only a few moments to spare, the modest commitment that Lent provides is a welcome respite from the seemingly endless expectations placed on people by work, family, bills, and societal norms, or by ourselves. For those who feel that they are treading water, never able to get ahead, Lent provides an ability to complete something over a relatively short period of time. Deanna from Arlington, Virginia, recalls that, in her younger days, she would commit to giving up chocolates but now, as an adult, "I'd rather commit myself to being a better, more compassionate person, which is what I do now instead!"[9] Her story reminds us that if one can conquer the little things of Lent, then perhaps we have it within us, with God's grace, to get ahead with those more expansive or longer-lasting tasks. Moderate commitment allows us a chance to be at peace with our humanity, our imperfections, and our exhaustion. Doing something spiritual for forty days, being disciplined enough to abstain from meat for six consecutive Fridays, or remembering to receive ashes can go a long way toward making sense of our otherwise overcommitted lives. Committing to these traditions for forty days can also open a person up to wider responsibilities, to longer commitments, and to feel more comfortable connecting regularly with a daily practice of prayer or being part of a community of faith.

4. RENEWAL AND RESOLUTION

The winter season, accentuated even more in cold northern climates, seems to draw many toward thoughtful introspection. Whether we can articulate this or not, early evening darkness and inclement weather often lead us to reconsider our life trajectory, reevaluate our choices, or in the days following Christmas, make a New Year's resolution. However, the routine of work, school, and other responsibilities in January can thwart our good intentions. Ash Wednesday, often only a few weeks beyond New Year's, can also serve as a new beginning, a second chance, and a fresh start. Lenten devotions provide a second take for broken or incomplete yearly resolutions. As Alexis from Wheaton, Illinois, notes, "Sometimes I like to think about Ash Wednesday as a redo of New Year's Day and as a second chance to make good on New Year's resolutions gone awry!"[10]

Lent serves as an opportunity for our personal renewal toward holiness—to assess and reform our habits or routines, to mend relationships with God and others. The first reading on Ash Wednesday (Joel 2:12–13) may tug at our conscience:

> Even now, says the LORD,
>> return to me with your whole heart,
>> with fasting, and weeping, and mourning;
> Rend your hearts, not your garments,
>> and return to the LORD, your God.
> For gracious and merciful is he,
>> slow to anger, rich in kindness,
>> and relenting in punishment.

While sitting in the pew, these words cut deep. We realize we may have neglected our relationship with God or fallen into a habit of sin along the way, yet the Lord offers us grace, forgiveness, and mercy. People participate in religious services on Ash Wednesday fully aware of their own fallibility. Perhaps, after weeks of winter contemplation, they have come to church for a moment to reflect on that admission and to grow in holiness. They may find it comforting that, in Lent, so many others are going through that process. Although this self-imposed scrutiny is deeply personal, they also know that they do not have to be alone in doing it. By joining those who are gathering in packed churches on Ash Wednesday, individuals may relish the anonymity, while also feeling comfort in knowing they are in the company of countless others.

They may not admit it, but those who reconnect with the Church during Lent are often fragile and uncertain about themselves, as true examination of conscience often can leave one feeling raw and vulnerable. They seek forgiveness and long for holiness. They crave mercy and absolution in this moment of renewal and resolution as they enter church on Ash Wednesday. This brokenness is not a feeling many can name at the time, but they long for an opportunity to start fresh and put the past behind them. Barbara from Mokena, Illinois, explains that, on Ash Wednesday, "I need to be reminded it is a time of forgiveness for me and others, it is a time to fast and pray, it is a time to rethink where I have been and where I may be going in relationship to the Lord and the Church."[11] The fact that ashes have a strong connection to many Christian funeral rites, where an officiant or priest says as the coffin is lowered into the grave, "Ashes to ashes, dust to dust," can be a humbling moment of understanding. The awareness of one's mortality can often lead one to repent for or reconsider past choices and commit to a path of renewal.

Those seeking a new start may feel that, if they can be true to a few simple but earnest promises for forty days, such as taking time for quiet prayer or refraining from online gossip, then perhaps they really can be a better, more holy person for the rest of the year or even longer. They seek another chance to prove to themselves, the world, and God that they can do it. Diana Hancharenko, the young adult minister at Saint Angela Merici Catholic Church in Youngstown, Ohio, observes,

[People] are more attuned with what they lack in life and seek a sincere desire for improvement. They want to be better people and seem to more willingly embrace opportunities for improvement [and see Lent] as the Church's invitation to do just that. Having a season built in for this purpose makes it more concrete for them.[12]

5. TRADITION AND IDENTITY

Ash Wednesday and the season of Lent occupy a special place in Christian history, deeply ingrained in our collective memories and experiences. Many people learn Lenten traditions in their families, as one generation imparts teachings and practices to the next. The rituals of ashes and meatless Fridays and the annual drama of Holy Week, for those who grew up with these elements, are often intertwined with a person's emotional connection to their parents and grandparents. For some, Lent is about honoring family.

Perhaps the tangibility of the ashes or the ease of understanding Lenten traditions have etched this season onto a person's consciousness. Perhaps the association between family and faith also plays a part in the strong attraction to this dimension of Christian tradition. No matter the exact connection, Lent has a powerful place within the Christian story. Even though terms like *ritual* or *ritualistic* may have negative connotations in secular society, there is still an attraction to them, especially around Lent. In his exploration of the meaning of ritual in an era increasingly detached from religious praxis, author Leonel L. Mitchell says that "we seem always more ready to reinterpret a ritual than to abandon it."[13] Perhaps ashes and meatless Fridays fall into this nexus wherein people seek new meanings for ancient traditions.

One of the responses I hear most often when asking people why they receive ashes is this: "Because I'm Christian—or, specifically, Catholic, Lutheran, or Episcopalian—and this is just what we do." Even if a person has not been to weekend worship for weeks or months, receiving ashes is seen as the expected Christian thing to do. Jacki, a self-described semi-active churchgoer from Chicago, notes that her annual Ash Wednesday tradition "has always been a way for me to start the Lenten season,"[14] and Nino, a Virginia young adult who identifies as nominally religious, does take time to receive ashes "as custom dictates and for religious observation."[15] Even though going to church or receiving ashes on Ash Wednesday is not required, there are a number of people who presume that it is and come because of this self-directed tradition.

It seems that, for many, Ash Wednesday participation is a practice done out of a genuine desire to be closer to God in the company of a faith community, rooted in a strong sense of spiritual identity. The introspection of winter can lead one to reflect on who they are—and Ash Wednesday and Lent are opportunities for people to rediscover that. Taking a moment for self-examination is attractive and can lead people to try an inward journey for the season. This is certainly the case for Cathleen, an individual with no religious affiliation (but who comes to churches on occasion) from eastern Pennsylvania, who says, "I miss the beauty and traditions,"[16] when thinking of the Church's rituals and traditions during the Lenten season.

Many people might also find comfort in the familiarity of Ash Wednesday and Lenten services. The practices in which they participate may be reminders of formative years when they or their parents may have been more active in church. Returning to the rituals first experienced in childhood may feel like a return to the security of a family's embrace or a constant, stable point in an otherwise chaotic world. The symbols and actions associated with Lent may remind some of who they were as a young person: optimistic, hopeful, excited, and free from the burdens of adulthood. This is similar to returning to childhood holiday traditions or revisiting the places, products, or pictures of nostalgic memory. Digging into one's personal story allows people to reset themselves in the right direction. Tapping into Lenten traditions, such as receiving ashes, fasting from meat on Fridays, or donating quarters for the Catholic Relief Services Rice Bowl, can connect people to their younger selves and to their core identity.

6. SENSE OF ACCOMPLISHMENT

When the stay-at-home order was in effect during the COVID-19 pandemic in 2020, my wife and I made the bed every day. Even though no one was coming over to our house, we took time each morning to tuck in the sheets, straighten out the covers, and organize the pillows. It was a daily domestic ritual, and nobody would ever see our handiwork. Why did we do it? It gave us a sense of accomplishment. Making the bed each day provided us with a feeling of having completed at least one task. For the rest of the day that followed, even if we felt defeated by our work, affected by health issues, or overwhelmed by our task lists, we still had one small victory. This simple and mundane act allowed the two of us to accomplish something, and that achievement was the motivation we needed to endure whatever arose in the hours ahead.[17]

For many, Ash Wednesday is just like making the bed in the morning. It's an uncomplicated routine, without needing prerequisites or extensive preparation. Yet, it gives the person who receives ashes a small sense of spiritual success. Each Lent, Fr. Greg Friedman, a Franciscan friar based in Albuquerque, New Mexico, reflects on wise advice from his spiritual director, who once told him, "If you would just do the things you are supposed to be doing—and aren't—that would be something good to do for Lent." Fr. Greg went on to note that he grounds himself in this task, saying, "Lent is about 'the basics' [and] 'the fundamentals,' which we need to renew and practice" every year that passes.[18] In today's world, simple endeavors like Lenten traditions can be oases in an overwhelming sea of seemingly endless projects, complications, or past failures.

In fact, the fear of failure is a very real thing, some of it fueled by the unbridled visibility we face in a social media–dominated world. Fear of failure can have surprisingly harsh consequences for our well-being. For some, "it can lead to debilitating anxiety and depression," notes Harvard business professor Arthur C. Brooks. "It can steer us away from life's joyful, fulfilling adventures, by discouraging us from taking risks and trying new things."[19] Sometimes, the dread of failure is brought about by perfectionism and avoiding anything that might disclose to the world our mistakes and shortcomings.

When it comes to religiosity, some feel they can do nothing right, that they are imperfect believers. They neglect to go to church services, don't read the Bible regularly, and forget to pray. Should they make it to church, these individuals are uncertain when to stand, sit, or kneel; where to find their place in the hymnal; or what words to recite at the designated time. Prayer can be a challenge as well, and they know they should make more time for speaking with God. Others struggle with giving to charity, worried about their own finances and well-being, afraid of letting go of their time or hard-earned money. Those who feel like religious failures do not often take risks or try new things when it comes to spiritual practices. They do not want to feel like a failure yet again, especially in church on Sunday when others, including neighbors or friends, seem to have it all together.

However, receiving ashes once a year is something tangible and personally fulfilling they can do to enrich their spiritual lives and leave church with some feeling of accomplishment. This is a day, perhaps known since childhood, when broken and imperfect people get to come to church. They take a small risk and depart feeling just a bit better about themselves. Corrine, a semiactive Catholic from Lockport, Illinois, notes that on Ash Wednesday she feels that she and others like her can "come together as a community with the knowledge we're all imperfect and that's okay," giving her a compelling reason to make the trek to church for ashes each year.[20]

This might all sound trite. For those who are more regularly engaged in religious praxis, this sense of accomplishment might even seem reductionist to the deeper meaning of Lenten traditions. However, for the person who regularly encounters failure, uncertainty, and being overwhelmed, receiving ashes is a big deal. Going into a church building, getting ashes, abstaining from eating meat for the six consecutive Fridays, or trying to give up chocolate, cursing, or beer for forty days are all significant accomplishments. Some may say to themselves, If I can do something like this for a day or a season, then maybe I can accomplish some of the more challenging stuff in life. Putting aside expectations or demands of perfection we sometimes place on individuals, we clearly can see that getting ashes is a minor, but also considerable, act of accomplishment, and the act has depth beyond our initial observation. The stories of these people are likely more complex than we realize at first glance, and there is no denying the victory of those ashes for one brief, shining moment.

7. BELONGING TO A COMMUNITY

If you were to walk through the crowded streets of a busy city on Ash Wednesday, you likely would notice many people with ashes on their foreheads—and as the day progresses, the number of individuals with this mark increases exponentially. Turn on the news that evening, and you may see newscasters, public officials, and interviewees marked with ashes. It's ubiquitous and pervasive: you cannot escape seeing it.

Catholic social scientist Dr. Mark Gray, who leads research at Georgetown University's Center for Applied Research in the Apostolate (CARA), notes that Lenten ashes are akin to the *I voted!* sticker one gets after casting their ballot on Election Day, "when people have an opportunity to wear their identities." He notes that those omnipresent stickers may actually lead to higher voter turnout.[21] The stickers serve not only as a mark of pride for engaging in one's civic responsibility but also as a great social marketing tool, reminding others to vote. On a deeper level, there is something about those markers that allows someone to feel like they belong to something bigger than themselves. In the case of the voting stickers, it helps people feel like we belong to our community or country. In the case of ashes, it helps us feel that we belong to God or to a particular expression of faith. Dr. Grey reflects on this:

> During Lent, in many ways, Catholics have opportunities to wear their religious identity. This contributes to their sense of belonging, where many other aspects of their faith may call more on their obligation to believe. On Ash Wednesday, your religious identity and sense of belonging is worn on your head. On Fridays, these are on your plate

(and then on Twitter, Facebook, and Instagram). Of course, this is just one aspect of the season, but it is important in the broader explanation of why U.S. Catholics become most active in their faith during this time of year.[22]

This *sense of belonging* cuts deep in the hearts of many people. Another social scientist, Dr. Josh Packard from the Springtide Research Center, has studied the increasing loneliness of young people and their strong desire for belonging. Springtide notes, "Durable, sustainable communities have always been built on a solid foundation of belonging....None of us can come together while so many feel left out."[23] In this research, Dr. Packard's team discovered that the disaffiliation crisis in religious institutions, especially among young people, is often due to their not feeling a sense of belonging when coming to church. And yet, for a brief moment on Ash Wednesday or while abstaining from meat on Lenten Fridays, people may feel they *do belong* to something and to someone. On a spiritual level, those who are active Christians know that this belonging is deeper than attendance or membership in a particular church, though that may aid one's journey of faith. We recognize that we belong to Christ, and the ashes, often in a shape of the cross, are a visible and tangible sign of the connection between the recipient and the one who died on a cross. Claudia, an active Catholic from Springfield, Virginia, affirms this sentiment: "I am branded for life that I belong to God!"[24]

When people see ashes on the foreheads of so many others, they may subconsciously be compelled to be part of a movement, as the *I voted!* stickers quietly compel us to vote. We want to engage with whatever has captured the attention of so many others, wondering if this might be a community where we can belong. "I think that joining in a communal practice helps solidify our membership in that community," recounts Bill, an active Catholic parishioner in Lowell, Indiana.[25] Brandon, who lives in central Florida, feels a common bond beyond his immediate family or friends, saying, "There's something uniting about seeing everyone's cross throughout the day."[26]

THE TYPICAL RESPONSE

The people who fill the pews on Ash Wednesday arrive with varying motivations, life situations, and degrees of religious practice. Each arrives at the church for a moment to begin their Lenten journey. But how do churches, and Christians in general, respond to this influx of people in the pews on Ash Wednesday? I have personally witnessed regular churchgoers react with frustration at the arrival of visitors and newcomers. I have driven in cars with fellow active Catholics as they pulled into the church parking lot and let out an expletive when they found all the good parking spots already taken and their preferred pew occupied by unknown faces. These experiences often fuel emotions as routines and habits are momentarily disrupted. They may feel slighted by a stranger or replaced by a rookie. Their own story is one of constant commitment. The Church has been a source of great comfort and joy in their lives. They come weekly and are involved in many parish activities, but suddenly, on Ash Wednesday, they are required to adjust and adapt. Even if their reaction is not conveyed visibly or audibly, they may fume inwardly—which can leak out in sideways glances, muffled whispers, or cold body language. Even when I stood in that long Ash Wednesday line around Saint Peter's in Chicago, I could sense the regular churchgoers were mildly annoyed by the fact that they had to stand outside on a cold Chicago day to get into a church they could easily enter at any other time of the year.

In talking with other active Christians about Ash Wednesday, I sometimes also get a sense of cynicism or nihilism. Some simply ignore the phenomenon or reduce these moments to fleeting experiences, believing this sudden anomaly won't matter anyway. Nothing changes, they say, and so it is not worth the time or energy to care more than necessary. On Ash Wednesday, I have seen them ignore newcomers or strangers, assuming these unfamiliar individuals will probably never come back. They prefer to nurture existing relationships rather than forge new ones that day. Connected to this are a few engaged churchgoers who view the sudden appearance of otherwise disaffiliated individuals with suspicion or distrust. They consider a stranger's attendance on Ash Wednesday as a probable façade and find it hypocritical for newcomers to think that ashes on their foreheads will suddenly make them holy, especially if they are already known within their neighborhood or community. Another reaction I have witnessed is much more inward in nature. They do not dislike, blame, judge, or disregard the newcomers on Ash Wednesday. In fact, in a purely benign way, they may not even notice them. Like so many others just mentioned, they have rich stories of faith, and the Christian community has been a blessing along their journey of life. Yet for them, Ash Wednesday is less about that larger, social community and more about their own interior examination of conscience, a private moment between them and God. That others are in the room, some new and other regulars, might just be irrelevant.

More often than not, a person who returns on Ash Wednesday is met with all of these individuals and responses. The common thread that runs through all of them, though, is the lack of engagement with the newcomer. Those who are not regular churchgoers will rarely interact with any other person on Ash Wednesday. Visitors then leave as they arrived: disconnected. Even in a packed church, the isolation is profound. If a person enters a church on Ash Wednesday with their frustrations, anxieties, nervousness, or uncertainty, and if the response (or lack thereof) from the active parishioner or member further exacerbates the heaviness, they likely will not come back again soon. Left within the isolation of their own thoughts as they reflect on these experiences, they may further disengage from the community and from faith itself.

AN ASH WEDNESDAY CHALLENGE

After vividly recounting the summoning of a community in the face of the oncoming storm, the prophet Joel offers his audience reassurance, found in the closing words of the first reading on Ash Wednesday:

> Then the LORD was stirred to concern for his land
> and took pity on his people. (2:18)

The biblical prophet speaks of the Jewish people, battered by years of wandering and exile, making their way back to the promised land. The divine response to this situation is concern leading to action, borne of God's compassion and love for his people, regardless of their past.

This is the challenge *we* are given as well: to be equally stirred to concern and driven to pastoral action when we witness the storm of crowds on Ash Wednesday and see how Lent draws so many people to conversion and holiness. We are called to offer *boundless hospitality*, to be like Abraham, who welcomed and gave his food and drink to three strangers wandering across the scorched desert who passed by the entrance of his tent (see Gen 18:1–8), and to follow the covenant of Moses, who reminded the Israelites before they settled in their new land, "You shall not oppress a resident alien...for you were aliens in the land of Egypt" (Exod 23:9). We are called to provide *radical warmth* in the manner of Jesus, who said, "Come to me, all you that are weary and are carrying heavy burdens, and I will give you rest. Take my yoke upon you, and learn from me; for I am gentle and humble in heart, and you will find rest for your souls. For my yoke is easy, and my burden is light" (Matt 11:28–30). And we are called to *unconditional compassion*, exemplified by the narrative portrait of the Good Samaritan (see Luke 10:29–37), the one who paused in the middle of his journey, moved by love and tenderness, to assist and accompany a stranger who was bruised, bloodied, and beaten.

Throughout Christian history, men and women like Francis and Clare of Assisi, Martin de Porres, Sojourner Truth, Damian of Molokai, Katharine Drexel, Dorothy Day, Dietrich Bonhoeffer, Martin Luther King Jr., Mother Teresa, Cesar Chavez, and Helen Prejean have taken up this challenge, were stirred to concern, and actively moved with boundless compassion, radical warmth, and unconditional compassion toward those bruised, bloodied, and beaten. In the sixteenth century, a penniless and eccentric Italian, Philip Neri, was so stirred to concern seeing the plight and poverty of his fellow Romans that he would strike up random and often joy-filled conversations of faith with total strangers in the streets and in the hospitals, warmly inviting them into deeper dialogue and fellowship. Without a doubt, it can be said that this path of pastoral concern is an integral part of the Christian story.

A few years ago, in the middle of a global discernment process the Vatican conducted, Pope Francis paused when he heard the tragic stories of young adults who were suffering and struggling around the world with poverty, migration, abuse, and more. In an apostolic letter that followed, he recounted the things that moved him to tears. "At times," he said, "the hurt felt by some young people is heart-rending, a pain too deep for words. They can only tell God how much they are suffering, and how hard it is for them to keep going, since they no longer believe in anyone." He then pivoted to a dream that all believers can work toward: "May all young people who are suffering feel the closeness of a Christian community that can reflect [Jesus's] words by its actions, its embrace, and its concrete help" (*Christus Vivit* 77).[27] After hearing the heart-rending stories that propel many to reconnect in Lent, we are now challenged *to care and be concerned for others*, to learn more about their stories, and to tend the wounds of the strangers in our midst. As Pope Francis encourages, "We can start from below, and, case by case, act at the most concrete and local levels, and then expand to the farthest reaches of our countries and our world, with the same care and concern that the Samaritan showed for each of the wounded man's injuries" (*Fratelli Tutti* 78).[28] In the same spirit, it's not so much about whether or not people will come to us but whether we will go out to them, wherever they may be.

Finally, we are called to *embrace the joy of new life and discovery*, grounded in the paschal mystery, that fuels hope in the future. Now that we have heard about this annual Lenten phenomenon, we can no longer ignore it. While it may seem strange, I personally find Ash Wednesday to be one of the most joyous occasions of the year. I get a chance to find God present in the hearts of people who are unfamiliar to me and who have yet to enter into my life. As I look forward to meeting these people, I am reminded of the wisdom of Pope Benedict XVI, who said, "Being Christian is not the result of an ethical choice or a lofty idea, but the encounter with an event, a person, which gives life a new horizon and a decisive direction" (*Deus Caritas Est* 1).[29] I recall the insight of

Archbishop Desmond Tutu who notes that "God made us for interdependence. A person is a person through other persons. This is when God rubs his hands in satisfaction and says, 'Yea, mon!'"[30] And I love the vision of Pope Francis who said, "The only way is to learn how to encounter others with the right attitude, which is to accept and esteem them as companions along the way....Better yet, it means learning to find Jesus in the faces of others" (*Evangelii Gaudium* 91).[31] In each of our Christian communities, we can choose to despair endlessly that people today are not connecting with faith traditions with the same frequency as they did in the past; however, realizing that Ash Wednesday is an annual occasion where those sobering trends get interrupted, we can see the possibilities of a new horizon and set off decisively in that direction. We are given a call to action to discover new life by finding Jesus in the faces and stories of those we are about to meet as they walk into our lives in Lent. Our call to action is grounded in a tangible hope that all is not lost and that there is truly something new and joyous that can emerge from the unfamiliar faces within our midst each and every Ash Wednesday, if only we are ready to take up this challenge.

FOR PARENTS AND GRANDPARENTS

In my years of pastoral ministry in the Church, I have encountered many parents and grandparents who are saddened as they watch their adult children disconnect from the practice of the faith tradition in which they were raised. The anguish of seeing them no longer come to church on a regular basis can be heart-wrenching. To these families, I offer a word of hope and encouragement. The fact that so many people are drawn to Lent and Ash Wednesday, and the fact that this act is often rooted in the tradition and lessons they learned from their parents and grandparents, gives me great hope. Even if they are not coming back to church for ashes or Lenten traditions, still have hope. If you instilled good values and shared your stories of faith with them through the years, those memories remain with them.

I encourage parents and grandparents to make a concerted effort to make someone else's son or daughter feel welcomed and loved in your community this coming Ash Wednesday. During Lent, extend the kind of hospitality, compassion, and joyful love to a stranger in your midst that you might provide for your own kin. Accompany them as you would walk beside a loved one. Make them part of your own extended family and help that individual feel as if they belong to something and someone special. Trust in the Lord that there may be someone out there who might be looking after your own adult son or daughter. As much as we would love to be the one who reconnects our family with the faith traditions of their younger days, there are times when this is just not possible. Rather than bemoan that reality, channel your energy to take care of another person in need of the love you offer.

Each year, we, as active Christians and leaders, are called to maximize the increased participation of so many people, especially younger generations, on Ash Wednesday and throughout the Lenten season. Pope Francis recently noted that "it is important to make the most of great moments of the liturgical year" to "provide a welcome break in [people's] routine and help them experience the joy of faith" (*Christus Vivit* 224). Perhaps, then, it is less of a challenge and more of an opportunity for all our churches. In an age when so many are walking *away* from religious institutions, we are encouraged to be more intentional and to pay greater attention to every person, one by one, who will be walking *toward* our communities of faith. Those who return on Ash Wednesday and Lent should have the blessed experiences of boundless hospitality, unconditional compassion, and joyful people who are waiting to meet and accompany them in discovering God's presence through refuge, renewal, commitment, accomplishment, holiness, tradition, spirituality, and belonging.

PRACTICAL IDEAS

Each of the following chapters begins with some broad principles and considerations, followed by a list of practical suggestions. It may be tempting to dive right into those ideas, but I encourage you to take the long view by brushing up on the principles, as they give the recommendations deeper meaning. In addition, there are specific ideas embedded in each chapter's opening half that you will not want to miss in your planning efforts.

The suggestions in the following practical ideas chapters are intended for consideration and implementation by active churchgoers, often in the leadership of their local Christian community—parish staff, church councils, pastoral ministers, and so on. There are obviously many proposals for ecclesial and church settings, but I have also included efforts that can be carried out in the home or within one's local community. For the pastoral leader, this means that the ideas presented can be both advice they can offer their congregation to do outside the church or suggestions for their own personal lives, as they accompany their own family, friends, and people with whom they interact in everyday life.

Chapter 3

PREPARING FOR A MOMENT OF RETURN

Call an assembly; Gather the people, notify the congregation. (Joel 2:15–16)

—from the Ash Wednesday First Reading

How can we get ready for Ash Wednesday? When should we start preparing? There is no better time than the present. The more we prepare, the better our response can be.

The response of the Christian community is an important component to the impact of a person's moment of return. Because the person returning is feeling vulnerable as they walk into the church, if they are met with indifference, suspicion, or even the slightest of aggression, the return could be short-lived. We are social beings and we put great stock in how we are perceived and received. When vulnerability is met with a lack of hospitality, people walk away. Therefore, it is critical for the parish community, especially active and regular churchgoers and the pastoral leaders within the community, to be *prepared* for these Ash Wednesday encounters and to adopt a spirit of hospitality and welcome for all those who gather that day.

Preparing for a Moment of Return

When the Day of the Lord is almost upon them, the prophet Joel summons together his own community, which we hear proclaimed each Ash Wednesday. He announces with vigor: "Blow the trumpet in Zion! proclaim a fast, call an assembly; Gather the people, notify the congregation; Assemble the elders, gather the children and the infants at the breast" (Joel 2:15–16). These verses sound as if they were delivered by a hurried mother, calling out with eagerness and urgency to every person in the home to prepare the house when she suddenly learns that they are hosting their entire extended family for dinner—and the guests are almost there.

Similarly, Ash Wednesday is always almost here. The entire family is about to be together again. Everyone in the house must prepare and respond when the time comes. This is the excitement, the nervousness, and the palpable anticipation that every church should sense prior to Ash Wednesday. To extend the previous analogy: We hope the soon-to-arrive extended family will not only stay for dinner but will want to move their belongings into the upstairs bedrooms and remain with us for a while.

In the second reading on Ash Wednesday, Saint Paul instructs the early Church at Corinth to be "ambassadors for Christ" (2 Cor 5:20). He proposes this responsibility to himself and to anyone who calls themselves Christian: to act as Jesus would act and to speak as Jesus would speak, much like an emissary would do in a foreign land or in conversation with those of another country or culture. Active churchgoers today can once again receive his message. We are challenged to act and speak as Christ would as we encounter other people, especially strangers and guests in our midst. The regular churchgoing community is challenged to step up to prepare for this day—to roll out the red carpet for those who will be arriving in droves.

The Center for Applied Research in the Apostolate at Georgetown University reports that, among all self-identified

Roman Catholics in the United States, almost half will come to a church or receive ashes in a parking lot, on a train platform, or at a community center next Ash Wednesday.[1] That is over forty million people! Furthermore, that number does not include the millions of Lutherans, Episcopalians, Methodists, Presbyterians, Baptists, and other faithful Christians who also honor this sacred day or the billions of people going through this rite in so many other countries around the world. This is certainly one very large family dinner that is about to take place. The guests are almost at the door. They are a new-found gift to our community. To receive this gift, though, we must be prepared. Just like the four anticipatory weeks of the Advent season prepare us to receive the gifts of Christmas, the community must also anticipate the arrival of individuals on Ash Wednesday with intentional preparation.

A NEW *SEPTUAGESIMA*

When the prophet Joel called the whole community to action, saying, "Blow the trumpet...proclaim a fast, call an assembly; Gather the people, notify the congregation" (Joel 2:15–16), everyone, from the elderly to the infants, was to step forward. No one was excused from this effort, not even the newlyweds on their wedding day. Although Joel was assembling his community in preparation for the onslaught of an invading army, the urgency can be carried over into our present circumstance. The entire parish community should be ready for immediate action when the crowds descend.

Prior to the 1960s, there was a Lenten preparation season within many churches' calendar years, called *Septuagesima*, which began seventeen days prior to Ash Wednesday. The word *Septuagesima* literally means "seventy," and it marked seven weeks (just under seventy days) before Easter. During this time, churches would begin removing flowers and decorations, and the priests and pastors would start wearing their purple vestments. Even the Alleluia was taken out of the liturgical rites a few weeks before Lent officially began. During the Middle Ages, the seventeen-day *Septuagesima* season was the time when consecrated religious sisters, monks, brothers, and priests would begin fasting. Fourteen days after that, on the last Sunday before Lent, local pastors would start their preparations. The laity were not obliged to commence their Lenten rituals until Ash Wednesday. Lay churchgoers would use *Septuagesima* as a time for consuming the balance of their meats and sweets so that their homes would be free from these items during Lent, giving rise to the Carnival and Mardi Gras feasting. The Second Vatican Council in the 1960s eliminated the *Septuagesima* season in order to point Christians toward Easter and the paschal celebration. As a result, the preparatory liturgical experience was lost. However, the *spirit* of this ancient season can certainly be retained today, especially among active churchgoers. As this short pre-Lenten period was the time for additional preparation among the faithful, it may be helpful to consider reviving a *Septuagesima* experience for the leaders in the faith community to anticipate and prepare for the arrival of visitors.

To reconnect with those who return to receive ashes and throughout Lent, it may be helpful for the parish or congregation to reflect on the aforementioned lessons of Joel and Saint Paul and develop its own *Septuagesima* experience. The pre-Lenten time of preparation, then, should be intentional and involve as many people as possible from within the active churchgoing congregation. This mobilization requires concerted time and effort on the part of church leaders to prepare active Christians for what to expect and how to respond, at church and at home. The initial planning for such efforts should begin, at least for organizers, in the autumn prior to Ash Wednesday; however, the involvement of the rest of the parish can ramp up just after Christmas.

SUGGESTED SCHEDULE TO PLAN AHEAD FOR LENT

Autumn or Before Christmas

✓ Begin making active churchgoers aware of the Lenten phenomenon.

✓ Work with staff, pastoral/parish council, and/or church leadership to coordinate the parish-wide preparation programs.

✓ Liturgical teams begin making Ash Wednesday liturgy plans.

Around Christmas and Epiphany

✓ Make active churchgoers aware of the Lenten phenomenon.

✓ Begin workshops and trainings for active churchgoers.

✓ Incorporate preparatory elements, prayers, and suggested ideas into parish small groups, sermons or homilies, and church communication, such as bulletins, emails, and websites.

✓ Pastoral/parish council discuss plans for welcoming newcomers on Ash Wednesday and make their Lenten plans with newcomers and guests in mind.

Three Sundays Prior to Ash Wednesday (*Septuagesima*)

✓ Pray for those who are struggling with their faith.

✓ Continue workshops and trainings for active churchgoers.

✓ Train ushers and greeters on how to welcome guests on Ash Wednesday.

✓ Train readers/lectors on how to proclaim the Scriptures throughout Lent.

✓ Post signs around church about welcoming guests on Ash Wednesday.

Preparing for a Moment of Return

Two Sundays Prior to Ash Wednesday (*Sextigesima*)

✓ Pray for those who seek acceptance and belonging.
✓ Continue workshops and trainings for active churchgoers.
✓ Send mailing to all registered members with ideas for Lent.
✓ Encourage churchgoers to invite friends and family to Ash Wednesday.

The Sunday Prior to Ash Wednesday (*Quinquigesima*)

✓ Pray for those who will come to receive ashes on Ash Wednesday.
✓ Pray for active churchgoers, that they may be radically welcoming.
✓ Center preaching around welcoming newcomers and guests.
✓ Challenge active churchgoers to be inviting and hospitable to guests.
✓ Post easy-to-read directional signs around the church property.
✓ Print worship aids, welcome guides, and sign-in sheets.

Because there is often a relatively short window of time between Epiphany and Ash Wednesday, this preparation of the community may be intense. Like Carnival season, this would truly be a feasting experience, as active churchgoers will be diving into potentially new and concentrated preparatory measures. Additionally, switching one's focus from the joy of Christmas to the sobering commemoration of Lent can be a challenge for almost anyone. Parish leadership should be thoughtful in navigating this preparatory time for the rest of the community. Despite these obstacles, the preparation of the parish or congregation is an essential component of this effort. Some internal discernment will be needed to determine what can practically be done within your local context and to what extent.

SIMPLE AWARENESS

The first step in this process is to simply make the community aware of the phenomenon that occurs on Ash Wednesday. It may seem obvious, but pointing out that many people will start reconnecting with the Church during Lent is very helpful.

Lent is often an inward-focused time, so it is natural that active churchgoers are primarily preoccupied with their own Lenten plans in the days and weeks prior to Ash Wednesday. Lent is also a busy time at most parishes, with additional activities taking place throughout the community—so church leaders and volunteers are also focused on those events. Bringing a kindhearted and optimistic awareness of this phenomenon is a great first step. A few suggestions for how this can be done include the following:

- **Raise awareness of Lenten participation** in sermons, homilies, and written reflections by the pastor or other leaders in the community in the weeks between Christmas and Ash Wednesday. Repetition builds awareness so it may be good to incorporate these insights on more than one occasion.
- **Encourage people to see the disconnection in their own families.** Much Lenten reconnection happens within the home (such as fasting on Fridays and giving up things for Lent). Invite active churchgoers to reflect on the experiences of their friends and families who may not go to

church regularly but partake in Lenten practices. Help them see that the people they know and love are often the ones reconnecting with faith practices. This can put a human face on an often-anonymous phenomenon.

- **Put up posters around the church,** complemented on the parish's website and on social media, with phrases such as: "They're Coming. Are You Ready?" or "Get Ready to Welcome" or "Who Will You Encounter This Ash Wednesday?" Post these in the weeks following Christmas and leave them up until Mardi Gras.
- **Share information about why people reconnect in Lent** (from chapter 2) in short excerpts in the bulletin or on the church's website in the weeks prior. This information can also be incorporated into small-group faith-sharing lessons between Christmas and Lent.
- **Invite parishioners to share their own stories.** Identify people currently active within the community who may have renewed their Christian faith on Ash Wednesday or reconnected with the Church during Lent. Ask them to share these stories during a Sunday church service, include it on the parish website, or post it in the bulletin. This allows other people to hear firsthand the impact of Lent and better prepare them for the individuals they may encounter on Ash Wednesday.

Another key aspect of the recognition process is developing *self*-awareness. Helping the community to know its own strengths and weaknesses as a place of encounter and refuge will go a long way toward preparing for the arrival of those who will reconnect with the Church in Lent. Consider doing a community-wide self-assessment that examines the vitality and viability of your church in order to better understand what newcomers will perceive about the place they are entering, some for the first time. It may be helpful for the congregation to go through this self-examination annually. Some questions for communities to consider:

- Within the current structure, where or to what ministries or individuals do new parishioners or young people often gravitate?
- How easy or difficult is it for a newcomer to understand the registration or membership process?
- What does the aesthetic of the church building say to someone who is new? Are there ways to improve or provide greater upkeep to the physical space?

There are various assessment tools that communities can use to measure their viability and organizational health. Some of these can be found in books and websites within a particular religious denomination, but it may be most helpful to work with someone—at a diocesan, national, or organizational office, or an individual church consultant. It is essential that the community go through some type of assessment process to raise this self-awareness and to know better what a new or returning person might experience upon their arrival in Lent.

SPIRITUAL READINESS

Since the medieval days of Christianity, the *Septuagesima* season began with the Sunday Gospel of the "laborers in the vineyard" (Matt 20:1–16), where the laborers who worked all day complained about the equal treatment given to those who had been hired a few hours prior. This parable seems somewhat fitting to the preparation for Lent, as active Christians and newcomers are equal on Ash Wednesday: all receive the same grace from God, regardless of their previous engagement with the practice of the faith. With this in mind it is expected that some active Christians may feel frustrated or angry when, after offering years of active participation in the life of the Church, those who have not been so active are given the same privileges on Ash Wednesday—and, as this book suggests, even recognized and celebrated. Therefore, the pre-Lent period should be an occasion to gently accompany regular churchgoers toward a spirit of compassionate, genuine, hospitable, and gracious evangelization. We must help all people be spiritually open to these grace-filled moments when others return.

Great sources of spiritual preparation are the messages of the Sunday readings during the time between Epiphany and Ash Wednesday. These readings can connect to preparing oneself to welcome and show mercy and compassion to newcomers and less active Christians during Lent. Sharing the spiritual insights of the Scriptures within the lectionary can be done in a variety of ways, including the following:

- **Homilies, sermons, or reflections**. While not to detract from the core teaching of the Scriptures on a given Sunday, which would be the focus of a homily or sermon, it is possible to make the connection for the parishioners for one, two, or all three Sundays prior to Ash Wednesday. These reflections can help the community respond to the call to be compassionate and merciful to strangers and newcomers; these messages hopefully would encourage active Christians to better encounter and accompany those who will arrive on Ash Wednesday.

- **Bulletin and website messages.** This is an easy way to connect the Sunday Scriptures and the call to missionary discipleship before Ash Wednesday; however, these may not always be read by the community. There may need to be a multifaceted communication plan for distributing these messages, including announcements at Sunday worship or on the church's website or social media pages.

- **Adult formation sessions** (Bible studies, adult education classes, prayer groups). Providing materials to adult groups that are already gathering is a simple way to offer spiritual formation on the value of welcoming and mercy. The community could also hold special one-time pre-Lenten Bible studies, prayer groups, or formation sessions with these materials already imbedded.

It should be noted that the exact dates for this pre-Lenten time leading up to Ash Wednesday will shift from year to year, depending on the date of Easter, a moveable feast, and the Sunday readings change over a three-year lectionary cycle. As a result, it may be difficult to present a consistent annual message related to pre-Lenten Sunday readings. Consequently, careful planning will need to be done by church leaders in advance of Lent each year. Spiritually forming active parishioners as compassionate missionary disciples, predisposed to welcoming newcomers on Ash Wednesday and throughout the Lenten season, and grounded in the Word of God is incredibly important.

One additional, and perhaps more consistent, annual way to prepare the community can be found in one of Christianity's oldest forms of prayer and reflection, *lectio divina* ("divine reading"), in particular around the Scripture readings for Ash Wednesday (see appendix 2). These readings have remained constant for centuries and across several Christian traditions. These annual Scriptures speak wonderfully to the reality of the moments of return that come on this day. One potential *lectio divina* plan or schedule is to reflect on the Old Testament reading (Joel 2 or Isa 58) four weeks prior, the Psalm (52 or 103) three weeks prior, the Epistle (2 Cor 5—6) two weeks prior, and the Gospel (Matt 6) one week prior to Lent.

This ancient spiritual practice involves a repeating recitation of the biblical passage in question (*lectio*), a reflection on its meaning and application to one's life (*meditatio*), a time of spoken prayer and conversation with God (*oratio*), and a contemplative silence to receive whatever God has in store for us through this process (*contemplatio*). Engaging the readings in this manner, while also reflecting on those who will come to church that day, can be an excellent and coordinated way for the community to spiritually ready themselves for the special moments of encounter on Ash Wednesday. As you or your community go through this experience, you may discover themes emerging, like boundless hospitality, radical welcome, unconditional compassion, the return of the exiles, our ambassador role for Christ, tradition and spirituality, renewal and refuge, commitment and community, among the many other topics that this book has raised to the reader's attention.

PRAYER AND ACTION

It may seem obvious, but an incredibly effective way to ready oneself for forthcoming moments of return is to intentionally and genuinely pray for those who are about to return. Whether at Mass each Sunday between Epiphany and Ash

Wednesday, in daily prayer and reflection, or in a community-wide program (like *lectio divina*, mentioned above), the habit of praying for and with those who are not regularly among us will be beneficial in orienting our hearts and minds toward the lived experiences of those we do not normally see.

This prayer, though, is not along the lines of this: "O Lord, please get these people back to church!" Rather, it is a deep and considerate prayer for whatever frustrates or pains them in their lives. It is a prayer for the human needs they have, whether that be relief from economic distress; eradication of personal suffering; elimination of racism and prejudice; healing from physical, emotional, sexual, or domestic abuse; maintaining or recovering the health and well-being of families and loved ones; clarity for the difficult choices they are making at work, in school, or at home; support for anxiety, depression, or loneliness; uncertainty on their spiritual journey; or whatever it may be. One reason disaffiliated persons have for not connecting with the Church is that they feel those in religious institutions do not care for (or pray for) them or their particular needs and that church organizations cannot possibly help them through challenging times. Therefore, a fitting pre-Lent prayer could be something like this: "O Lord, please help these individuals with whatever they need in their lives right now. Be with them, Lord. Guide and comfort them. And put me where you need me to be along their path."

Parishes can coordinate this prayer effort by working with active Christians who have loved ones who have disengaged from the practice of their faith: sons and daughters, parents, cousins, brothers or sisters, colleagues and co-workers, neighbors, old friends, and so forth. Invite parishioners to submit those names and some of their needs (for the sake of privacy, only first names should be provided) and ask other active churchgoers in the community to spend the three weeks leading up to Lent praying for one of the people named. Even if the individual lives elsewhere, it can be a blessing to know that someone somewhere is praying for them. Similarly, it can be comforting for active parishioners to know someone in their own parish is praying for their family or friend. This coordinated effort can predispose the community to look upon those who are not normally active with gentle compassion.

Identifying the disaffiliated person's name and praying for their needs can also inspire regular churchgoers to address the issues that afflict so many people. Like others, those who are disconnected from the practice of the faith struggle with issues like poverty, injustice, unemployment, abuse, racism, mental and physical health, isolation, and other concerns. In addition to coordinating the prayer effort, church leadership can provide opportunities for members to get involved with social justice issues that impact those who are not regularly engaged. Working for justice within these important areas might also allow active parishioners to connect directly with less active Christians in the community—to listen to their needs, hear their stories, and dialogue with them. Any activity like this, though, is not about recruiting people to come to church or fixing their problems; rather, it is aimed at seeing and being present for others, to encounter God already at work in others' lives, no matter their current religious praxis. And very often, entering the lives of others, experiencing their situations, and meeting Christ present in their hearts and souls can be transformative for us and our communities too. Local churches can coordinate these efforts in the weeks or months leading up to Lent, so that, when a visitor enters church on Ash Wednesday, the community is receptive to them, can better understand their situations, and can be more responsive to the realities they experience.

WORKSHOPS AND TRAINING

Pastors and church leaders can prepare active members to know more about those who will be joining them in greater numbers in Lent, as well as teach them effective outreach, invitation, and accompaniment practices. Knowledge of those who are disaffiliated from the practice of the faith may be limited to our personal experiences with friends or family members who are no longer practicing. While this firsthand awareness is important, as it grounds the situation in familiar territory, it is also important that churchgoers understand the vast diversity and breadth of the population they may encounter on Ash Wednesday. It would be incorrect to assume that everyone who walks into the church that day has left or has returned for the same reasons as one's own disaffiliated family or friends (see chapter 2).

Further, encounters with newcomers on Ash Wednesday can be delicate, intimidating, or awkward. Because of that, it is helpful to provide active parishioners with an explanation of and training in effective practices of interpersonal relationships, invitation, and outreach with and to those who return. Churches should discern which format would best serve their people and choose to use more than one option for presenting information. This includes new formats and technologies that are yet to be developed; therefore, it is important to make use of the latest media platforms available at any given time. Communities may choose to

- **host presentations.** These could be held on one or more weeknights or during the day on one or several weekends in the weeks leading up to Lent. One topic could be examined in-depth, or multiple topics could be done as a series of presentations over several weeks.

- **train active churchgoers.** Training workshops could provide hands-on experiences, wherein people actively engage in recommended practices in outreach and evangelization. These may be a one-time training or a series over a week or weekend before Lent.
- **host webinars.** An online, interactive presentation may be offered once or more during the period before Lent, allowing churchgoers an opportunity to learn at home. Integrate small-group discussions and interactive conversations to allow for dynamic dialogue and participation.
- **produce a video series.** Parish leaders can record videos on various topics and post them on the church website or social media platforms and email them to active parishioners. This is especially helpful for those with busy schedules, as the videos can be seen at a time convenient for the viewers.

Trainings and workshops may address some of the following topics:

- **Who is coming on Ash Wednesday?** Using national and local data, this session could provide an overview of the populations who reconnect with the Church in Lent, including the disaffiliated and young adults. Furthermore, it may be helpful to present the rich cultural diversity that exists today, especially among younger populations and demographics with which the local parish may not be as familiar.
- **Why might people return for ashes and during Lent?** Recognizing the diversity of reasons why

61

individuals reconnect with their religious roots in Lent (see chapter 2) is important for parish communities. Understanding the reasons behind the return, as presented in this session, may make parishioners sensitive to the needs of newcomers and be better able to respond.

- **How do we accompany others in Lent?** Knowing how to journey with those who return to the practice of the faith on Ash Wednesday or in Lent is a skill worth sharing. This session could provide a better understanding of and best practices in radical hospitality, compassion, accompaniment, and missionary engagement of others.

In any of these trainings or workshops, it would be good to mix presentation with interactive discussion among parish leadership on the aspects most relevant to the community, as well as by identifying churchgoers and members and those outside the community who may have particular expertise in these topics. The presentations can be led or facilitated by the pastor or his pastoral staff, by active parish leaders, or by experts from the ministerial, ecclesial, or academic fields. Ideally, these sessions should be held in the weeks following Christmas. The most crucial element of preparation is providing a greater awareness of the people who will be returning to church during Lent, so that the preconceptions or assumptions about those individuals are not the foundation upon which communities rest.

INTENTIONAL INVITATIONS

It may seem counterintuitive to invite even *more* people into an otherwise crowded space, but that opportunity presents itself in the weeks leading up to Ash Wednesday. While many people do come to church on the first day of Lent, there are even more who are not returning at all. Just as Christmas and Easter services are often promoted in newspapers and on social media, the same can take place prior to Ash Wednesday. Consider being bold and invitational about these opportunities throughout the local community. Sharing news or opportunities for the upcoming Lenten season can also be done in partnership with restaurants known for meatless dinners, such as pizza, pasta, seafood, salads, vegan food, and more, or those owned or operated by church members. Perhaps use social media to make Ash Wednesday and Lent go viral in the local area, raising public awareness of the opportunities that await people at a nearby church. Complementing this, however, the most effective invitational action that can be done in anticipation of Lent is personal engagement. Actively, intentionally, and gently inviting friends, families, neighbors, and colleagues to join in an Ash Wednesday experience will go a long way. Personal invitations should be a natural progression of a fruitful relationship already in place.

In their national pastoral resource for evangelization, *Living as Missionary Disciples*, the Catholic bishops of the United States suggest a fourfold methodology for a personal invitation process: (1) encounter, (2) accompany, (3) community, and (4) send. This method is based on four of Jesus's key instructions to his disciples to "come and see" (John 1:46), "follow me" (Matt 9:9), "remain in me" (John 15:4), and "go, therefore, and make disciples of all nations" (Matt 28:19).[2] This process gives excellent guidance for extending intentional invitations for Lent:

- **Encounter.** The first step in making an invitation is to see the face of Christ in the person being invited. It may be tempting to pass judgment on a person's lack of regular engagement with a faith community or presume to know the reasons for their estrangement. Instead, it is important to see Christ alive in them as a son or daughter of God, seeking grace, hope, and peace. Whether we have known them all our life or if our acquaintance has only recently started, encountering them anew by seeing the Lord within their life story rekindles the relationship, strengthens it, and allows it to go deeper.

- **Accompany.** The key to being invitational is listening—lots of it. Recognizing that our presumptions may be wrong, the sensible next step is to ask and dialogue with the person: What gives you joy? Where do you struggle? What do you think about faith and about Church? What is it about religious institutions that concerns you? Simply listening to and entering into their stories can teach us something about them and also provide insights about faith and life that we may not have recognized before. Accompaniment is a gradual, often slow process as we all follow the Lord, so we must also practice this patience ourselves.
- **Community.** People want to feel accepted for who they are and to have a sense of belonging. They want to know they are not alone in this world, that others genuinely care for them, and that they can remain in the Lord's company. When speaking specifically about young people, Pope Francis has noted that they "need to be approached with the grammar of love...spoken by those who radiate life, by those who are there for them and with them" (*Christus Vivit* 211). In

this spirit, would the person being invited feel accepted or that they belong if they accompanied you into the community holding the Ash Wednesday liturgy? Would your own presence convey that? If so, then an invitation could be extended with full confidence.

- **Send.** This final step in the process of invitation is to go out boldly (but always gently) and extend a personal invitation to participation on Ash Wednesday or on another occasion during Lent. Because of the high engagement of other disaffiliated people throughout the Lenten season, the thought of reconnecting with the faith community at this time may already be in the back of their mind. Additionally, if the person has truly felt encountered, accompanied, and fully accepted by you, this invitation to them as a fellow disciple will be the natural next step in this journey of faith.

We are inviting our loved ones to a time and a place of rest, a time of renewal, and an opportunity for belonging (among other things), all of which are critical to those who experience uncertainty, pain, and a feeling of being overwhelmed in their lives. In the Scriptures, Jesus extends an invitation to the besieged people of his day: "Come to me, all you that are weary and are carrying heavy burdens, and I will give you rest" (Matt 11:28). This should be the same kind of invitation we make to those we encounter and accompany "with the grammar of love" (*Christus Vivit* 211). When making any kind of invitation, it is also key to be intentional about using the person's name. The value of being known and called by name is important for the individual being invited and welcomed, especially in a culture that prefers anonymity. The most effective invitations are often the ones that are the natural product of growing relationships we have with others, not just a quick or impersonal invite to an upcoming event or group. In short: be genuine, patient, and loving, with an honest interest and concern for the invitee's life experiences and story.

LITURGICAL AND LENTEN PLANNING

In any given year, once the Christmas decorations are stored away, the focus of parish liturgical leaders moves to Lent. The tone of the music in choir practices begins to shift away from the *Gloria* and *Alleluia* to something more reflective and introspective. The purple fabrics, often just retired from Advent, are washed and readied for display once more. The parish scheduler may begin to incorporate the Stations of the Cross into the mix for upcoming Friday evenings. Even amid these annual practices within the brief weeks after Epiphany, parishes and local congregations can think anew in order to make the upcoming encounter with crowds of newcomers a truly momentous occasion for them and for the church.

While the specifics of planning for Ash Wednesday will be covered in the next chapter, during this pre-Lent moment, be sure to put careful effort into all the planning of liturgies and parish schedules, always keeping in mind those who may be experiencing these annual rituals for the first time or after a long while. This means a greater consciousness about our church customs or traditions that may be familiar to regular parishioners but largely unknown by those outside the community. For instance:

- **Provide explanations**. First and foremost, we cannot assume that everyone who comes to church on Ash Wednesday or Lent will know the routine. Plan to explain things in a way that makes sense to someone unfamiliar with parish or universal Lenten customs, while also avoiding a condescending tone in the explanation.

- **Mark church entrances.** Do not assume that people will know which door to enter upon arrival in the parking lot. Many churches have multiple entrances and possible options for navigating the church property. Consider large directional signs and outdoor greeters on Ash Wednesday to help those who may be new. Similarly, keep in mind how a newcomer might navigate from the front door to the pew or main sanctuary, and plan accordingly with signage and ushers.

- **Select familiar music.** When choosing musical selections for Ash Wednesday and the first Sundays of Lent, plan familiar songs rather than hymns or liturgical settings that are brand new to the assembly or known only to the most regular churchgoers of your parish or congregation.

- **Prepare worship aids.** While many people know that Ash Wednesday is important, they may not necessarily know what to do to receive ashes upon arrival in the church or when and how to say the various prayers during a Mass or worship service. Consider preparing a printed or electronic worship aid or guide, explaining the rites and rituals of the liturgy that day, as well as in the early weeks of Lent.

- **Train lectors and readers.** Proclaim the Ash Wednesday readings in a way that engages listeners. This is important! While the lectionary readings are repeated each year, consider that some people may be hearing them for the first time. The Church has placed these readings into the Ash Wednesday liturgy to move people toward reconciliation with God and a renewal of spirit, and good proclamation can convey that message in a dynamic way.

- **Coordinate greeters and ushers.** In advance of Lent, prepare those individuals who are serving in a hospitality role (volunteers, ushers, greeters, check-in hosts) with plenty of tips and suggestions on how to welcome newcomers. Include some friendly suggestions on interpersonal engagement. On Ash Wednesday, it may be tempting for these individuals to be overwhelmed with the crowds and lose their patience with an uncertain or curt visitor. Offer in advance suggestions on keeping cool under pressure and avoiding displays of unnecessary aggression or frustration. Recognizing that this can still happen, church leaders need to make plans to pastorally care for greeters and ushers before, during, and after Ash Wednesday with affirmation, moments of rest, and a listening ear. Another concern is that some ushers and greeters could get caught up with conversations with one another or with people they already know, thereby missing new people as they enter. Addressing this habit could be helpful so that these benign oversights have less chance of occurring as the visitors arrive.

- **Consider schedules.** Plan Lenten events that are accommodating to people's lives and schedules, especially those who are very busy or overwhelmed with domestic responsibilities. We cannot assume that a congregation's or parish's customs will have the same appeal to newcomers and those less active in the community. You might also consider scheduling special events during Lent for specific audiences, including those who are returning after a long while, those who are going through difficult times, those in their young adult years, and other groups.

The key is to make an intentional effort to gear the local Lenten experience, from the liturgy to the schedule, toward those who are less active. Such work will go a long way toward making the environment a welcoming and hospitable one that a person would want to return to again and again. Those who are already engaged in the parish or congregation may not even notice the difference—and that is okay—but regardless of those observations, these measures will truly make the experience better for everyone.

A NEW STORY

The practical preparation just listed will be very helpful in transforming Ash Wednesday and Lent from moments into milestones, but one thing remains: the personal openness to having our own story radically changed. No matter how many workshops we have or how well-crafted our liturgies might be, if we are not open to having our lives upended by the inclusion of another human story intersecting with our own, then it will all be for naught. This personal preparation is the crucial ingredient, as it is often in interpersonal encounters that churches and religious institutions have both driven people from the pews and created a sense of true community and love. Above all else, we must each *ready ourselves* for what is about to come.

During the days before Lent, or, for that matter, throughout the year, it is important to reflect on how our current story is about to change, both personally and communally. Before a recent national dialogue process to better engage youth and young adults conducted by several prominent Catholic organizations, planners drafted a "way of proceeding" to guide these conversations and interactions. This "way" included important considerations for healthy discourse such as the demand for mutual respect; the advice to not fix, save, advise, or correct; the suggestion to "turn to wonder" if feeling defensive or judgmental at any time; the reminder to be mindful of body language; and the encouragement to trust and learn from silence. In so doing, the "way of proceeding" prompted participants to be fully present, to listen without a need to respond, and to be humble before the sacred story of another human being.[3]

In a similar way, before we proceed any further into implementing these preparatory steps, here are some suggestions that truly prepare us for the wondrous encounter that will unite our story with another's story—and potentially reshape both.

- **Reflect on your own story**. First, reflect on your own journey, and on the moments where you have felt heard and appreciated. Who mentored and guided you through life and faith? How was your own world upended when you immersed yourself into your spiritual life and into the community of faith that welcomed you in? What God-given gifts were you and are you still able to contribute to your church? Consider these and other reflections on your own story.

70

Having this sense of self can be helpful as, in the encounter you may have with another, you will need to be open to sharing your story if you want a newcomer or visitor to trust you and feel at home with you and your community.

- **Forget everything you think you know.** As already said in various ways, to truly enter this experience, we must put aside our preconceptions. We do not know why someone has come to church on Ash Wednesday or during Lent. We do not know how their journey has led them to this moment. We do not know the struggles and pains of their past. Forget everything you think you know and be ready to encounter each person as they come. Respect the mystery and their individual story.

- **Take time to listen to the stories of your family and friends.** Practice the art of encounter and accompaniment by more carefully listening to the stories of the people you already know and love: your family members and friends. Not only will such acts enhance your existing relationship with them, but it can also remind you that there is always something new to learn.

- **Stop to encounter the stranger.** Going beyond your close friends and family is the next step in the process of preparation. Even in the busiest of times during your day, stop what you are doing at that given moment and make time for someone you do not know well: the cashier at the store or the receptionist at your doctor's office; the mail carrier or express delivery person; the person in the office, in your neighborhood, or at your child's little league games you always see but have never spoken with; or the person in line next to you at the supermarket, while on vacation, or getting coffee. Making the most of these little encounters reminds us that every soul we meet has a story to tell, and to unlock that story, we simply need to stop and open the door.

- **Find ways to connect another's story to your own.** Always look for common threads in the stories you hear to link your experience with theirs. This is not to reframe the conversation back to you, as it should always be about the other person; rather, this is to help make an authentic connection with another person. This enables us to recognize that the experience of others is not that different from our own. When we discover this, it allows us to make empathy our default mode.

- **Be responsive when people are in need.** Whether it is the homeless person we pass on the street, or someone in the school or workplace who looks like they could use assistance, be always ready to respond. We should make a habit of being more aware of those in need around us and respond in kind. Having this mindset will prepare us to be equally responsive and compassionate on Ash Wednesday and throughout Lent.

When the prophet Joel mobilized his community to prepare for the oncoming storm, as we hear on Ash Wednesday, he desired that it would be a time for every single person to step forward to act. The same is being asked of active Christians in advance of Lent each year. Through prayer, formation, listening, and planning, the community members can ready themselves so that a newcomer will truly feel at home.

Preparing for a Moment of Return

Saint Paul uses a particular phrase in the second Ash Wednesday reading: "Working together, then..." (2 Cor 6:1), which evokes the notion of "co-workers," a concept Saint Paul also uses to describe his relationship with fellow missionaries like Apollo (see 1 Cor 3:5–11) and Timothy (see 1 Thess 3:1–2), who worked alongside him to advance the gospel in the early Church. In a way, Saint Paul now calls out to churchgoers already in the pews to "work together, then" in preparing for an encounter with so many wonderful and new people in Lent. By embarking on this campaign of preparation, the experience of Ash Wednesday will be even richer in whatever community takes on this responsibility; working together, then, with each other in service to the stranger that will walk through their doors on Ash Wednesday, just imagine what is possible because of that encounter.

Chapter 4

THE ASH WEDNESDAY EXPERIENCE

> Behold, now is a very acceptable time; behold,
> now is the day of salvation. (2 Cor 6:2)
>
> —from the Ash Wednesday Second Reading

The church is packed! We have been preparing and we are ready to go. Now that Ash Wednesday has finally arrived, what should we do today?

The typical Ash Wednesday experience is often this simple: After walking or driving to a church, a person enters the front doors and finds a seat or stands along a wall. As the service begins, they listen and participate as they are able, get in line, receive ashes, and either return to their place or head out the doors. A few of the visitors may stick around longer, but when the service is finished, most quickly leave the church and return to work, school, or home.

In recent years, the experience has become even shorter. For a growing number of people, Ash Wednesday involves driving into a parking lot on a mid-winter day, rolling down the window, receiving ashes and a blessing, rolling up the window, and driving away. Or maybe they wait in a long line on a city block, inching toward a church, going to a designated spot, getting ashes, turning around, and heading back to work. For a few others, their experience might be walking over to a priest or minister on a train platform who makes a sign of the cross in ash on their forehead, after which they go about their days. No matter the specific circumstance, the stories are often rather uneventful, unmemorable, and uninspired. A person can experience this ritual without saying a word to anyone. A regular churchgoer can have a similar experience, but they are more likely to get a nonverbal recognition or a cursory greeting from someone they know going through the same motions. In some instances, a person encounters a frustrated and exasperated volunteer, staff member, or pastor, who makes them feel completely unwelcome—and they walk away. But what if something different happened?

What if, on Ash Wednesday, a newcomer were greeted warmly at the door when they arrive or when they walk up to a minister? If they are in a church, perhaps they are escorted to an available seat by a friendly usher. Just maybe, in that instance, when they sit down, the person to their right or left might engage them in light conversation or, at the very least, offer a friendly smile and introduce themselves. What if, as the service begins, the space, the music, and the prayers all gave the visitor a profound sense of rest and refreshment? What if a sermon, reflection, or homily caused the newcomer and the regular churchgoer alike to experience a wondrous mix of comfort, insight, and challenge? What if everyone in the church that day truly felt connected to one another as they all received ashes together? And what if, at the conclusion of that moment, a newcomer wanted to stay around even longer? Perhaps everyone who received ashes that day was excited to come back again. *What if?*

This is no fantasy or imagined contrivance. These scenes are not only possible for any community, but they have also happened before. This *what if* scenario, adapted to one's local circumstances, should be the goal for every church and Christian community on Ash Wednesday. James Behan, a pastoral leader in the Archdiocese of New Orleans, recalls how he stepped into this experience:

> When I was a campus minister, Ash Wednesday was, hands down, my busiest day and most important day of the school calendar as that was the day I encountered the most students, staff, and faculty of the college or university. If God was going to whisper to them, "Come back to me," then I was going to be darn sure I was modeling tenderness, mercy, and compassion.[1]

Like James, we can write a new story. We can make the typical Ash Wednesday experience, that unmemorable and monotonous ordeal, a relic of the past and chart a new course. Saint Paul declares at the end of the second reading of the day: "Behold, now is a very acceptable time; behold, now is the day of salvation" (2 Cor 6:2). Ash Wednesday is indeed an eminently acceptable moment to change the story; *now* is the day of salvation.

There are four major elements to consider on Ash Wednesday: the digital component, the arrival, the experience itself, and the epilogue. These four elements can provide the foundation for a fresh narrative, where a newcomer or visitor will depart the church feeling they truly belong—they are valued and appreciated, supported and loved—and will want to return.

THE SETTING
Throughout this book, the word *church* is often used as the default term to describe the setting

of the Ash Wednesday experience; however, the location of ash distribution may be done in a variety of places. This can include a community center, church basement, school or college campus, parking lot, train platform, subway station, office building, hospital, military base, a person's home, or other places. While many Ash Wednesday rites around the world are done in churches, they do not necessarily need to be. These events can range from a ritual that includes Eucharist or it can be a two- or three-minute encounter with a priest or lay minister. As you read, please be aware of these distinctions. You may need to substitute the correct location or duration for your circumstances. In this book, there are some specific callouts or references made to several of these various scenarios in which ashes are distributed; however, adaptations can be made as your tradition allows. What is essential is that more intentionality be placed on whatever format or structure your community or denomination has established for the imposition of ashes.

THE DIGITAL COMPONENT

With the prevalence of social media, people share almost everything online. From posting snapshots of a delicious meal to disclosing the welcome news of a child's birth or a thrilling job transition, we, as a postmodern culture, love to share. It should come as no surprise that Ash Wednesday and the hashtag—#ashtag—trend across all social networks each passing year.

According to John Grosso, the digital media director for the Catholic Diocese of Bridgeport in Connecticut, "The curious thing is that Ash Wednesday has 'trended' differently depending on the social media phenomenon of the day." He notes that, over the past decade, he has witnessed how ashes have not only survived but evolved and thrived in the sophisticated algorithms of Twitter, Facebook, and Instagram. "We see the highest engagement rate on all our [diocesan social media] platforms from Ash Wednesday through Lent and Easter....The most heartening thing for me, though, is how intentional people are online during this time....I think we flock to digital spaces in Lent because we are drawn to a community as we journey together through this season."[2] Social media influencer and Catholic priest Father Rafael Capó of Miami shares a similar sentiment: "People seem to enjoy watching the expressions of faith coming from all sectors of society, from all ages and professions, and in a particular way, seeing personalities, politicians, actors, and VIPs expressing their faith on Ash Wednesday. It's cool to show your faith on Ash Wednesday."[3]

On Ash Wednesday, as people turn to their mobile devices or scroll through social media, they begin to see friends—from active churchgoers to those less active in their faith—post selfies with ashes on their foreheads or sharing details about their #AshWednesday experience. These posts remind social media users to visit a church or seek out someone distributing ashes on their way to wherever they are heading. As the day goes on, the social media posts continue populating their feed and they are reminded yet again to receive ashes. Before the day is done, they, too, may contribute their own selfie, #ashtag, or insights into the digital milieu.

Some might scoff at this idea, believing that such posts betray Jesus's own teaching about prayer and fasting where he says, "Beware of practicing your piety before others in order to be seen by them" (Matt 6:1). In fact, this very gospel passage is proclaimed in most Christian churches on Ash Wednesday. So, shouldn't we be discouraging, rather than encouraging, such a digital trend? I would argue *no*. The digital sharing of ashes is part of the notion of *belonging* that people seek on Ash Wednesday. By adding their voice or image to the social media collective, individuals are connecting to a larger family and claiming solidarity with millions of others around the world who are doing the same thing that day. Of course, flaunting overt piety for praise and adulation should be avoided; however, when most people post their #ashtag, it is not for self-glorification. They simply want to be part of something bigger than themselves.

Some suggestions for encouraging and accompanying people online include the following:

- **Prepare in advance.** In the weeks leading up to Lent, host one or more training workshops for active churchgoers on how to use social media and digital resources in relation to their faith. These sessions can be opportunities to explain terms and functionality and provide tips on effective, compassionate use of social media. Additionally, churches can run weekly tips on digital engagement in their bulletins, weekly communications, and web pages. If your church has certain guidelines and regulations regarding Lenten practices, you may consider posting those online (up to and including Ash Wednesday or the Fridays in Lent) with kind notes that encourage an invitational approach to your denomination's fasting and abstinence traditions.
- **Coordinate the hashtags.** Posting Ash Wednesday selfies and updates using #ashtag is a common occurrence and, in many cases, happens

79

naturally. It may be good, however, to coordinate or announce this and other hashtags before or during your ashes service, to draw attention to your community, thus allowing church leaders to track its direct impact that day. Post the specific hashtag you will be using on Ash Wednesday in your bulletin, weekly communications, and web pages.

- **Encourage selfies and posts**. Rather than leaving it up to chance, actively promote the use of selfies and Ash Wednesday posts on social media among your active churchgoers. This promotion will need to be explained carefully to avoid bragging, grandstanding, hypocrisy, or sacrilege; however, when people know that their church leaders are comfortable with and supportive of social media sharing, they may be more likely to do it themselves. However, it is also important to know the appropriate time to take these photos. For instance, it is highly discouraged to take selfies or snapshots during the liturgy itself; rather, if this idea is to be encouraged by the local congregation, it should be carried out *after* the Ash Wednesday service is finished.

- **Ask people how they are doing**. On Ash Wednesday, when fasting and abstinence requirements are paramount in people's lived experiences, ask how they are faring or surviving the fast. This concern reinforces that we do care about one another and their situations. Matt Kresich, a church minister in Cedar Lake, Indiana, posted his internal thoughts on a recent Ash Wednesday and invited others to share how they were doing. In his post, he shared some of his own humorous reflections on the experience, including, "I'm not a breakfast person, but I really crave it on fasting days" and "I am spending an above average time mentally figuring out what constitutes a snack."[4] Ask people what their full meal of the day included, share your meatless meal, or offer your own favorite meatless recipe.

- **Propose compassionate invitation.** When encouraging the use of social media, it is especially important for church leaders to communicate that a person's tone and words matter. In addition to avoiding bragging or hypocrisy, we must also use our digital voice in welcoming and compassionate ways. Consider ending an Ash Wednesday post with something like: "I hope that you, too, might find a place of rest and a community that will walk with you."

- **Collect email addresses.** As you encounter people on Ash Wednesday, whether at a church or at a pop-up ash distribution point, invite people to share their email addresses, social media handles, or mobile numbers, if they feel comfortable doing so. This can be through sign-in tables, cards in the pews, digital registration tools, or simply letting people know you would love to keep in touch. Having contact information like this will be helpful for building relationships beyond Lent's first day. You may also consider small quarter-sheet flyers with the contact information of spiritual mentors or directors, parish ministers, or pastors in the leadership of the community. Some who are suspicious of sharing their information upfront may be more willing

to take your leaders' contact information home
with them.

- **Don't limit it to one day.** While social media
trending of Ash Wednesday is wonderful, the
hype often goes away by day's end. Consider
ways to stretch the digital conversation into
Lent and beyond. If email addresses, social media
handles, or mobile numbers are collected, send
out regular communications, inviting people to
additional opportunities. On social media, use
hashtags and announcements that keep newcomers invested in your content. You may want
to encourage Lenten challenges or invite people
to share updates on how their fasting is going or
unique ways they have found time for prayer or
almsgiving.

THE ARRIVAL

There are just as many ways for a person to arrive as
there are ways that individuals receive ashes. Regardless of the
circumstances, individuals must be met with radical welcome
and hospitality. In recent years, pastoral leaders across several
Christian denominations have even taken that hospitality to
yet another level: They have gone out from their churches to
meet people where they are. One popular initiative, called
Ashes to Go, was formally started by an ecumenical group
of clergy, representing Episcopal, Presbyterian, Disciples of
Christ, United Church of Christ, American Baptist, and Men-
nonite traditions, in St. Louis in 2007. This effort involves
standing on a street corner or wherever people pass by in
their daily routines and, one by one, distributing ashes, offering a moment of prayer, and simply being available for fur-

ther conversation, should the recipient want to talk more. The *Ashes to Go* movement has since spread across the country, reaching California, New York, and Illinois.[5] Reflecting on her pastoral ministry in the greater Chicago area, Episcopal priest Reverend Heidi Haverkamp reports how many young adults and disaffiliated individuals she encountered while distributing ashes on train platforms and church parking lots. She notes, "People were crying as we gave them ashes and prayed with them through their car window."[6] What made these moments so profound is that the recipient's arrival was greeted warmly, with unconditional kindness and compassion.

Wherever ashes are distributed, depending on the norms and customs of your community, it is essential that the welcome and encounters are warm and sincere. As we do not yet know that individual or what they have experienced prior to the encounter, we are called to treat them with the highest regard. Every single person who arrives on Ash Wednesday is our *guest* and should be welcomed with utmost regard, no matter their story or past. Saint Benedict of Nursia, the great Christian monk who lived in the fifth and sixth centuries, laid out a strict rule for his religious order regarding strangers who arrived in their sacred space: "All guests who present themselves are to be welcomed as Christ, for he himself will say: I was a stranger and you welcomed me (Matt 25:35). Proper honor must be shown to all."[7] Many centuries later, in a much more secular setting than a monastery, American entrepreneur Walt Disney made sure every person who visited Disneyland would be called a *guest* rather than a tourist, ticket holder, customer, or attendee. This tradition continues to this day in every Disney theme park and institution around the world.[8] As Nicole Perone, a national leader working with young adults, notes in her appreciation of Ash Wednesday, "The response a faith community has to those moments of return or gateway moments can make or break it, and must be abundantly hospitable and inclusive [and] utterly joyful at the presence of each and every person."[9]

Taken together, the example set by Benedict, Walt, and Nicole encourages us to do no less: treat every person we encounter on Ash Wednesday as our honored guest. Recalling the words of the prophet Joel in the first reading that day, "Blow the trumpet in Zion! Proclaim a fast, call an assembly" (Joel 2:15), put another way: "Roll out the red carpet." Yet, do this without embarrassing a person or calling undue attention to their presence. Here are some suggestions for extending radical hospitality to those who arrive uncertain of themselves:

- **Take ashes to the people.** If your church allows for this practice (please check with your pastor or bishop), consider using the *Ashes to Go* model (https://ashestogo.org/) and distribute ashes within your local community in places where people often gather or pass by. If you use this model, ensure that the imposition of ashes is not transactional, like picking up a meal in the drive-thru, but leads to deeper prayer, conversation, and an invitation for further engagement.
- **Host off-site prayer services.** If your church allows, you may consider hosting an Ash Wednesday prayer service at an alternative location in the area such as a college campus, community center, nursing home, military base, prison, library, park, beach, office building, or residential common space. Be sure to get permission from whoever oversees these spaces. Services in the community allow people to receive ashes wherever they may be, especially if their schedule does not permit them to attend a Mass or worship

service in a church. The prayer experience should be brief and accessible for those who are unfamiliar with this Christian custom.

- **Make church parking easier.** With larger crowds on Ash Wednesday, church parking lots can get overwhelmed very quickly. Assign volunteers to direct traffic and make the parking experience easier on everyone, whether they are a newcomer unsure where to park or an active churchgoer who finds their normal routine upended. The traffic attendants should also be smiling and friendly to everyone who pulls in.
- **Greet people as they arrive.** This is essential to the radical hospitality experience. As people walk into the church building or a worship space (or wherever ashes are being distributed), have greeters ready to welcome them. Approach those arriving with a friendly smile and express gratitude for their presence. It may be necessary to have enough greeters on hand to ensure that each person receives personal attention. While it can be tempting to catch up with familiar people, be sure to instruct greeters to never neglect a new guest. Nonetheless, discreetly assess the context of each situation. For instance, if a guest does not seem interested in deep conversation, it is best to allow them their space while gently inviting them in.
- **Call people by their names.** It may seem simple but being called by name goes a long way toward feeling seen and acknowledged, especially in an unfamiliar space. Anyone encountering a guest upon their arrival should introduce themselves and, in so doing, invite them to share their name.

Once known, it is important to use that name throughout a given conversation.

- **Gather names and prayers.** Your church may consider collecting the name, contact information, and prayer requests of each guest who arrives on Ash Wednesday. This can be done in a variety of ways: a sign-in sheet filled out upon arrival; small cards in the pews along with pens or pencils; through a mobile app; or on the parish website. So that newcomers do not feel singled out, encourage every person in the community to do this. This information gathering not only provides contact details for newcomers but also offers a way to know what community needs to pray for and about throughout the Lenten season. Be kind and accommodating, however, if a guest does not wish to share their contact details for privacy reasons.

- **Accompany people to their seats.** If one is hosting an Ash Wednesday service of any kind where seating is involved, walk with guests into the worship space and either offer an available seat or simply let them know where they are welcome to sit. The spiritual accompaniment process we hope to initiate with a guest sometimes begins with the simple act of literally walking a few steps with them. During that short journey, if appropriate, the usher can engage the person in friendly conversation with the goal of making them feel as comfortable as possible.

- **Look around you.** As a society, one of the bad habits we have in public gatherings is avoiding eye contact. Rather than talk *to* people, sometimes we talk *about* people. Ash Wednesday is a great time to break that habit and begin looking (but not staring) at our fellow guests who have come to receive ashes. Ask regular churchgoers to acknowledge those seated near them with a nod, smile, and, as appropriate, an introduction. On this day, each of us has arrived seeking something; even as our stories are different, our paths have converged this day. Look around with kindness and joy at the people whose paths have wonderfully collided with yours on this special day.

- **Give up your favorite seat.** In an act of radical hospitality, consider surrendering your favorite seat to a latecomer or a guest whom you do not know, especially if no seats are available. They may be feeling exhausted as they hurried to church. Their feet might need some much-needed rest, and you could easily offer that for them by the generous act of giving up your own preferred pew or chair.

- **Help those who look confused.** If the people seated near you on Ash Wednesday appear unsure of what to do, consider helping them. A phrase like "Don't worry. If you need a hand, just follow me." Hearing "I'm happy to help" may be a relief to someone unfamiliar with the rubrics. If a worship aid or order of service is available, ensure that each guest has one and knows on which page the service will begin.

- **Provide Ash Wednesday welcome cards or guidebooks.** Whether your community is hosting a prayer service or Mass or distributing ashes in parking lots or street corners, offer every guest a printed welcome card or guidebook to look through during the experience and to take home with them. This guide may include an explanation of Ash

Wednesday, the order of worship, and answers to some frequently asked questions, such as "Do I have to be a practicing Christian to receive ashes?" "What do I do or say when I receive ashes from the minister?" or "When do I stand, sit, and kneel today?" Add a positive note of gratitude for all present. The card or guidebook can reiterate and reinforce—in print—the hospitable spirit of the community. It might be a one-page card or a small booklet; it should be more than an information sheet, a bulletin, a hymnal, or a missalette, but rather something special and unique for Ash Wednesday. A community might also consider including a note of invitation to upcoming activities. Be sure to list the church's website and the contact information of a church leader available to the guests in the coming weeks.

THE EXPERIENCE ITSELF

The experience of receiving ashes has been around for thousands of years. It is a basic act rooted in the religious traditions of ancient peoples. Its constancy and simplicity have likely been what kept it going for generations. The formulas used by many Christians today as ashes are imposed upon their heads, such as "Remember you are dust and to dust you shall return," "Repent and be faithful to the gospel," or some variation thereof, are modest expressions that can either remind us of our mortality or challenge us to embrace the divine. While these fundamental elements are core to the experience and should not be changed, the rest of the experience surrounding them can certainly be developed and shaped to truly impact those who have come.

The Ash Wednesday Experience

In the Catholic Church, the Roman Rite encourages reception of ashes within the context of a Mass or a Liturgy of the Word; however, allowances may be made for distribution outside of a church, such as visiting the sick or without a full liturgical experience. In Episcopal, Lutheran, Methodist, and other mainline Protestant communities, services that include the imposition of ashes often are offered on Ash Wednesday; however, pastoral leaders are also free to distribute them in other settings, as appropriate. Regardless of denomination, the ritual often includes a combination of all or some of the following: the entrance rites and greeting, reading of Scriptures, a sermon or homily, petition prayers, an offertory, communion rites, and concluding prayers. At some point within these components, ashes are distributed.

Sometimes, however, these ritual elements can confuse or disorient Lenten visitors. Knowing exactly when to stand, sit, and kneel, or remembering precisely what to say or do at any given point of the service can be intimidating. To a newcomer, the possession of this religious knowledge seems something only a few select people have. This uncertainty is one reason why some individuals opt to depart the church after receiving ashes or simply disengage for the remainder of the service. One might worry whether they are not holy or sinless enough to truly partake. Without a clear understanding or a helpful explanation of the rubrics, it makes sense why less active churchgoers could think this. Their sudden departure from the sanctuary may not be borne from laziness, irresponsibility, or a transactional desire to get their ashes and leave. Rather, it may involve deep-seated feelings of unworthiness, self-doubt, or not wanting to embarrass themselves by messing up the seemingly complex liturgical rituals.

Additionally, when speaking with people over the years, I have found that a memorable homily or sermon either illuminated or frustrated the faith life of a person in the pews.

This includes Kelly, a semiactive young adult Catholic from Washington, DC, who recalls, "In college, I attended services on Ash Wednesday tailored to the struggles and relevant issues among college-aged students....I found this meaningful and authentic."[10] To this day, she continues to search for experiences like this or an Ash Wednesday message that truly connects but has yet to find one. That singular occasion years ago was indeed a powerful moment.

The work of church leaders, then, is to avoid causing any unintended moments of fear or shame and to amplify messages with authenticity and meaning. Whether a Christian community is offering a brief prayer in a public space, holding an extensive liturgical service, or anything in between, the following suggestions may be helpful for enhancing the essentials of the moment and making people feel more integrated into the ritual experience:

- **Give clear directions.** If confusion is part of the distance between active and less active church-goers, provide verbal instructions or explanations throughout the liturgy, which may be complemented by a card or guidebook at their seat or displayed words on a screen. Even a friendly announcement from the pastor or worship leader, such as saying, "Please feel free to sit," or "We invite you to stand," can go a long way toward making someone feel comfortable in their next movement.

- **Create a sacred space.** There is great power in ambiance and environment. The beauty and aesthetics of a spiritual destination can elevate a pilgrim's heart and soul. Similarly, the church or location of ash distribution itself should be an uplifting place. Take great care during Ash

Wednesday preparation to create a sacred space, so that guests can be transformed by what surrounds them that day. Without developing lavish displays that would betray the simplicity of the season, consider various elements of art and environment that can be adjusted to allow for feelings of sacredness and illumination. These may include the desert or barren motif (i.e., leafless trees, dry bones, etc.), bowls of ashes, purple cloth and altar décor, banners/signs with key messages, and instrumental or meditative music.

- **Sing familiar songs.** If music is used on Ash Wednesday, consider selecting pieces that are either easily sung or familiar to most people. Complex hymns can discourage a newcomer, as well as a regular churchgoer, so the first day of Lent may not be the time to include those selections. Using well-known songs, such as "Amazing Grace," that are familiar offer comfort or renewal and complement the readings and spirit of the day (and "Amazing Grace" is indeed well-suited to Ash Wednesday).

- **Lean into the readings.** The fact that the same Scriptures are used on Ash Wednesday every year and across almost all Christian denominations should cause us to explore more deeply these biblical passages. In addition to *lectio divina* reflection in preparation for Ash Wednesday (see chapter 3), the community may wish to incorporate the messages and words of the prescribed readings (Joel 2 or Isa 58, Ps 51 or Ps 103, 2 Cor 5, and Matt 6) in various ways. This may include displaying or projecting them or incorporating them into banners in the sanctuary.

The presider may also wish to weave them into the introductory comments or petition prayers in the liturgy or unpack them more fully in the sermon or homily. The actions of the congregation that day should further reveal the meaning of the readings. Furthermore, all the readers or lectors, including the presider and cantor, who are assigned to proclaim the readings of the day should be well-trained, properly prepared, and fully engaged to deliver the biblical texts with appropriate emotion. Through the proclamation of the Word, they can invite the assembly to listen more attentively to the biblical stories, leading the congregation to imagine that they are hearing these words directly from Joel, Saint Paul, the Psalmist, and Jesus for the very first time.

- **Lead with Jesus.** The forty-day time frame of Lent is meant to mirror Jesus's journey into the wilderness, and each week's successive readings in the lectionary recount significant events in the Lord's story (the temptation in the desert, the transfiguration on the mountain, the encounter with the woman at the well, the raising of Lazarus, and the triumphant entrance into Jerusalem). The whole season culminates in the dramatic experience of Christ's passion, death, and burial—and leads into his resurrection at Easter. The fact that Lent is wrapped intricately into the human story of Jesus may be a major draw for many guests. In whatever way possible, on Ash Wednesday, *lead with Jesus*, or to put it plainly, put priority emphasis on the person of Christ in preaching, art, environment, print materials, and more, allowing individuals to connect their personal struggles with the struggles of the Lord.

- **Share your own story.** The season of Lent is a journey each person in a Christian community passes through—from the bishop or pastor to the individual who has never been to church before. Each year, we return to Ash Wednesday anew, shaped by our individual faith stories, which we can share with one another. Whether in a conversation in the pew with a guest, in the sermon or homily, or in a reflection shared by a layperson, consider ways to tell the story of your journey. It can remind a newcomer that they are not alone in their struggles, uncertainties, and doubts—and that we all have our faults and failures. If we expect guests to be open with us, we must also be vulnerable with them through telling our stories.
- **Offer a compassionate message.** On Ash Wednesday, it is essential to project a feeling of compassion, warmth, and welcome in every component of the liturgy. Tone matters, and it is important to keep in check the way in which the presider or readers speak. The message of the sermon or homily should not be an exhortation against past failures but rather an invitation to live up to our best selves. Recognize that many guests are already aware of their sins and shortcomings, so be gentle in the words shared. When addressing a crowd of unknown faces or speaking with a new person in the church on Ash Wednesday, it can be tempting to make a seemingly harmless joke or inference at the expense of visitors. However, this could be damaging to the listeners' souls. For

instance, it may seem natural to note that some people in the pews that day are unfamiliar to us or point out that it was hard to find a parking space. These lines may get a light chuckle from a few active churchgoers, but to the newcomer, it feels as if they were just called out. Keep in check these and similar microaggressions; avoid unnecessary jokes at the expense of others; and always speak with kindness.

- **Savor each encounter.** When we distribute ashes, we should treat each person with utmost respect. During distribution, it is easy to rush from one person to the next, as if the congregation were an assembly line. Instead, take each encounter as a liminal experience. Look into the eyes of the person with love, touch their forehead or sprinkle ashes above their hairline, and intentionally say the prescribed words with sincerity and emotion for every single person. Katie from northwest Indiana recalls that, when she distributed ashes one year, "I not only had tears in my eyes, but to look into the eyes of so many people and see their soul shine through was incredible."[11]

- **Invite a newcomer to distribute ashes.** One idea for radical hospitality is inviting someone new to assist with the distribution of ashes to others. This may be someone that you met before services or with whom you have an initial conversation. Invite this guest to help the church with the ritual, giving them instructions on where to stand and what to say and, if they accept, making sure they are supported. By giving them this experience (or simply making the offer), we are saying, "We trust you and we believe in your leadership abilities"; in so doing, they may find how meaningful it was to distribute the ashes and grow closer to God and your community. You should also let them know that it is perfectly fine to decline this invitation if they wish.

- **Humbly invite people to remain.** If your liturgy continues beyond the imposition of ashes, consider sharing a humble invitation immediately prior to the distribution. This offer should not be conveyed in a guilt-inducing manner or as a reminder of obligation or expectation. It should acknowledge that the rites that follow are an opportunity to meet and connect more deeply with Jesus and to further reflect on all our shortcomings with the support of a loving community.

- **Pray for their needs.** Consider including the lived experiences of the guests in the petition prayers offered during the liturgy. This may include economic situations, mental health concerns, racism and exclusion, exhaustion, stress, worries about family and the future, and specific needs that have arisen within the local area. If custom allows, invite the congregation to speak aloud their personal intentions. Hearing their own concerns expressed in these prayers will join the visitor's internal prayers with those of the community and allow them to feel seen and understood.

- **Allow for silence and rest.** One of the primary reasons people attend services on Ash Wednesday is the search for peace in an otherwise noisy, complicated, and overwhelming world. Throughout the liturgy, allow for intentional silence and restfulness. Perhaps it is already embedded in the rites of your tradition; regardless, it may be helpful to name this aloud during the service—to acknowledge that we all need to slow down and allow God to gently speak to us through the silence.

- **Offer practical challenges.** Another reason for the increased engagement in Lent is the desire for renewal and a fresh start. The Ash Wednesday liturgy can be a ritualistic expression of that desire. With that in mind, it might be helpful, during the Mass or worship service that day, to offer some practical ideas and modest challenges for the season of Lent (and beyond). If people are willing to come to church on Ash Wednesday, they may be willing to step up to another challenge or opportunity for action. Recall one of the reasons for reengagement is "a sense of accomplishment." Make an invitation for another achievement. Even more, there is great importance in *verbally* sharing these suggestions rather than limiting them to a church bulletin or website.

- **Conclude with another invitation.** Both at the start and at the conclusion of the Ash Wednesday service, invite those assembled to remain after or to return later in the week (i.e., that Friday or next Sunday). The invitation should not be heavy-handed, but further enhance the expression of belonging that the arrival, accompaniment, and liturgical experiences should have already conveyed that day. See the next section and chapter 5 for ideas on what those invitations can point toward.

TENDING THE SHEPHERDS: SUPPORT FOR CHURCH WORKERS ON ASH WEDNESDAY

During and after many Ash Wednesdays, pastoral leaders have shared with me their own stories about the beginning of Lent. Some share the joy they have experienced when seeing new faces and having special encounters with individuals at their local church. However, there are others who express frustration and exhaustion at the crowds for which they felt unprepared. During Ash Wednesday services, they may have felt taken for granted or maligned by guests. As Benedictine priest Adrien Nocent notes in his reflection on the season, "Lent is, most basically, a time of care for the soul. Newcomers to the faith are not the only ones who must be concerned with the growth of their own soul; every [Christian], however long baptized, must have the same concern."[12] It is important to challenge ourselves to be hospitable, compassionate, and joyful toward newcomers; it is also critical to tend the shepherds and active churchgoers and to provide internal support for pastors, pastoral staff, secretaries, volunteers, greeters, ushers, and other people who interface with the individuals who make moments of return on Ash Wednesday. These measures could include the following:

- Panning intermittent breaks for volunteers throughout Ash Wednesday
- Establishing a special break room for use between services
- Letting staff and frontline workers know they can safely express any anxiety, frustration, or anger in confidence with key leaders
- Offering support groups for dialogue about these experiences

- Equipping staff and front-line workers with mental health resources
- After Ash Wednesday, hosting one or more programs of gratitude for those who planned and staffed those liturgical experiences

THE ASH WEDNESDAY EPILOGUE

One of the unique characteristics of Ash Wednesday is that it has no other accoutrements. The prayer services and liturgies of Christmas and Easter, two other major Christian moments of return, are often accompanied by family gatherings, holiday brunches or dinners, or traversing across town or across the country to enjoy the remainder of the festivities. But Ash Wednesday is different. Depending on the situation, people may have time immediately following a liturgy or after receiving their ashes that day or later in the evening. This is an opportunity to invite them to more.

If guests do not see the value of Christian community and regular engagement in the traditions of faith, their departure on Ash Wednesday may mean a lost connection for another year. To secure their attention for a few moments longer, however, could mean all the difference in the world. If a person is willing to remain for at least fifteen or thirty more minutes after the formal liturgy ends, the likelihood of them returning for another occasion greatly increases. This is because, at that moment, we have offered them a sense of belonging and acceptance into our community. They matter to us and we have demonstrated that. Here are some creative suggestions on what to do as an *epilogue* to the experience:

- **Giveaways.** As people depart, provide something tactile that people can take home. This could include a small cross or a statue of Jesus; a bookmark or prayer card; a devotional or prayer book; a box for collecting spare change and dollars for those most in need (such as the Rice Bowl from Catholic Relief Services); or a sticker they can post on their laptop or water bottle. These tokens can help extend the experience beyond Ash Wednesday and the worship space, reminding people of their time with you for the remainder of Lent (and beyond).

- **Meet and Greet.** The church can host an informal social gathering with light beverages and healthy foods in line with the simplicity of the day. Both active churchgoers and guests can mingle with their neighbors and fellow worshipers after the service concludes. Introductions and icebreaking questions might include the following:

  - What do you do for a living? What is your course of study?
  - Where do you live? Where do you work?
  - What is your favorite thing to do or place to eat in this area?
  - Who is your favorite athlete/team (or artist, author, or actor)?
  - What brought you to this church (or to receive ashes) today?

- **Soup and Small Group.** Invite people to join for thirty or sixty minutes of small-group conversation over the Ash Wednesday readings or topics like What should we give up for Lent? or What are your favorite Lenten traditions? Provide some meatless food choices, bread, and light beverages to complement the dialogue.

- **Prayer and Listening.** In a small group over some refreshments or a simple meal, invite people to share one or two things for which they wish for others' prayer or support. Take time in those small groups for quiet or guided prayer. These groups can also be a forum for listening to the needs or creative ideas of participants. A facilitator may ask questions such as What in the local community most concerns you? or How can our church best respond to the situations in our world today? or What can our church do to better support people in need? Allow participants to respond.

- **Short Presentation.** In a relaxed setting, a member of the community or a noted speaker can provide a brief talk on a current issue or a topic connected to Ash Wednesday or Lent. An interactive question-and-answer session or dialogue can follow.

- **Church Tour.** At the conclusion of the formal liturgy, the pastor or a pastoral lay leader could lead a short tour of the worship space, giving deeper description of the building's layout, history, artwork, design, and liturgical elements. The tour should be interactive, allowing for questions and offering friendly, easy-to-understand explanations. A newcomer may feel more comfortable in your worship space if they had a richer appreciation of the environment and its story.

- **Meatless Dinner.** The community can host a simple meatless dinner (fish, pasta, soups, pizza, or vegetarian dishes) after the Mass or service without a formal conversation or presentation. If a religious community does not have Lenten fasting or abstinence requirements, then this meal could include meats, desserts, and other foods; however, even in these cases, simplicity is always preferred as it complements the austerity of the season.

- **Service Project.** After the Mass or worship service, participants can serve together on a charity or justice project, either on-site at the church or at a nearby location such as a soup kitchen, shelter, nursing home, prison, juvenile detention center, hospital, park, or thrift store. If held at the church, guests there could prepare or organize nonperishable food items and donated goods, make calls or write letters to legislators on social concerns, or send packages to military personnel or prisoners. Any of these are an excellent engagement in Lenten almsgiving.
- **Keep Connected.** For all these aforementioned ideas and post-liturgy gatherings, be sure to make note of who participated through a sign-in sheet or mobile app. This information will be essential for the days and weeks that follow.

In all this talk about the large crowds of people who come to church on Ash Wednesday, we still cannot forget about the many others who have opted not to connect. Some people may not trust the Church, others might find little relevancy in its rituals, many could be simply overwhelmed in the middle of their week, and a number may have never been invited. Regardless of the reasons, part of our Ash Wednesday "epilogue" should include going out to these individuals, perhaps on the Thursday or Friday of that first week of Lent. Keep in mind that it is not always about why people are not going to church, but how the Church can go out to them and meet them where they are. There are many other resources available about this. What is important is that we never forget the person or persons who are not there and do our best to be present for them, wherever they may be.

For many believers, though, Ash Wednesday remains a powerful occasion in their lives. "Behold, now is the day of salvation," shouts Saint Paul to us in this day's readings (2 Cor 6:2). Yet this day—this sacred moment—can grow even deeper and create lasting roots for the guests who come, regardless of how often they otherwise attend church. To achieve this wondrous goal, it is incumbent on every Christian community to put forth a greater sense of intentionality, compassion, and purpose in carrying out Ash Wednesday plans: in our digital spaces, at our doors, in our liturgy, and in all that follows.

Chapter 5

THE LENTEN JOURNEY

Working together, then, we appeal to you not
to receive the grace of God in vain.
(2 Cor 6:1)

—from the Ash Wednesday Second Reading

Once Lent begins, what can we do next? How do we build
on the initial moment of return and engage people for the
subsequent forty days? The possibilities are endless.

While we see large crowds descending on churches
throughout Ash Wednesday, it is much more difficult
to observe the multitudes of people who are abstaining
from meat on Lenten Fridays and the many who are giving
up something or doing positive acts for the season. These
numbers are often unnoticed because Lenten traditions are
usually practiced out of public view compared to the visible
presence of churchgoers filling the pews on Ash Wednesday.
Aside from a person's social media posts about the practice,
few would know if someone were giving up chocolate or
alcohol or limiting their screen time during the six weeks of
Lent. Most devotional practices are carried out in private—at
home, at work or school, in daily routines, within one's personal

reflection, and during family occasions. It seems the Gospel reading for Ash Wednesday truly is lived out during the forty days and nights that follow: "Whenever you pray, go into your room and shut the door and pray to your Father who is in secret" (Matt 6:6). With these instructions on prayer, fasting, and almsgiving, we move from Ash Wednesday and into Lent, having received our marching orders from the Lord himself. We try to keep our Lenten praxis quiet, unassuming, and low-key. But the inevitable sometimes happens. We falter, forget, and wane. We begin the season in earnest, with a strong commitment to keep our promises. As the weeks wear on, the discipline to pray, fast, and give may become more difficult. Abstaining from meat one day per week is a modest commitment (and an opportunity to try other foods), so it makes sense why this Lenten custom is common. Other practices, however, may quickly become a chore, especially in our inner rooms, behind shut doors, and done in solitude and privacy. It is challenging to do Lent alone.

In the Second Letter to the Corinthians, which we hear on Ash Wednesday, Saint Paul implores his listeners, "Working together, then, we appeal to you not to receive the grace of God in vain." (2 Cor 6:1). What stands out are the words *working together* (in Greek Συνεργοῦντες[1] which means *synergistically*), a phrase Saint Paul uses to describe his co-workers in the service of God along his travels (seen in 1 Cor 3:9 and 1 Thess 3:2). By these very words, he is recommending that we do not journey alone as we move toward Christ. We need co-workers and companions to keep us moving forward, lest we falter, forget, or wane in our commitments or stumble on the road before us. Going further, Saint Paul appeals that we not "receive the grace of God in vain." By working in synergy with one another, by supporting and encouraging our fellow Christians, all of us—from the most active churchgoer to the most recent Lenten visitor—can avoid receiving our Lenten graces in vain and remain faithful to our prayer, fasting, and almsgiving.

The Ash Wednesday readings, then, prepare believers for a season of Lent that is both personal and communal. Further, that community element can be done in a cooperative spirit of pastoral support and synodality (a centuries-old church word, also rooted in Greek, that means *journeying together*). Looking at our current Lenten phenomenon, active church-goers are challenged to accompany the numerous individuals who live and work within their local neighborhoods and cities, many of whom are journeying alone this Lent, perhaps even faltering or waning in their own way without the support of a loving community of faith.

In speaking about communal support of youth and young adults, Pope Francis recently said that "the community has an important role in the accompaniment of young people; it should feel collectively responsible for accepting, motivating, encouraging, and challenging them" (*Christus Vivit* 243).[2] He was clear that no active Christian is excluded from the responsibility of looking out for others; rather, all should treated "with understanding, appreciation, and affection, and avoid constantly judging them or demanding of them a perfection beyond their years" (§243). While this was spoken about younger generations, the same principle can apply to those of any age bracket, for we are all sons and daughters of God. Just as the community is called to prepare for those who would return in Lent and warmly welcome the guests they met on Ash Wednesday, so, too, is the community encouraged to accompany individuals throughout the season of Lent and beyond. This can be done by understanding others' situations, appreciating their presence and giftedness, and freely extending our compassion and affection.

OPEN TO GROWTH

The high levels of Lenten engagement may also point toward a genuine openness of many to the spirituality and growth of the forty-day season, including those persons who are less connected to regular religious practice. Those who give up sweets for Lent or have meatless meals on Fridays are likely the same individuals who receive ashes. For some, that may be their only church attendance that year. Therefore, there is a natural connection between the first day and the remaining days of Lent. The invitations offered at the end of a person's Ash Wednesday experience, as described in chapter 4, can lead to a deeper commitment in the weeks that follow.

One of the blessings of Lent is that it gives us over forty days to get it right. The prophet Jonah gave the people of Nineveh forty days of fasting to sit in sackcloth and ashes and repent for their sins (Jonah 3:4–6). This is a good amount of time to accept God's challenge, to make an intentional plan of action, and to move closer to God. Growth takes time, and forty days are a sign of the Lord's gift of patience for us. Another analogy for this season is *spring training* for major league baseball, which often occurs simultaneously with Lent on the Christian calendar. During this time, players renew their exercise and routines, getting back in the habit of throwing, catching, and fielding so that, when Opening Day arrives, they feel confident and energized to make it through the long regular season that follows. The scores from the spring training games do not count, so players can work through their mistakes without penalty. This allows athletes to *get it right* in much the same way that Lent offers us the necessary time to perfect our own routines of prayer, self-sacrifice, and social engagement. For many guests (and maybe ourselves), there may be a misconception that we only grow from Lenten practices when we accomplish them perfectly, when we never falter from fasting, or when we do not wane in our commitments. These misunderstandings prevent many from truly getting to the heart of the season. Instead, we are called to help one another, just like a community of Ninevites or a baseball team in spring training. "Iron sharpens iron," Proverbs states, "and one person sharpens the wits of another" (Prov 27:17). So, too, are we called to do for each other throughout Lent.

THE PASTORAL APPROACH

People who reconnect with Lenten traditions are often struggling or uncertain, so they must be approached with gentle and pastoral care. Most of those who avoid church are not actively working against the Christian faith. They are often not atheists or agnostics who want to argue with churchgoers over their morals or beliefs. Whether they have intentionally disengaged or slowly drifted away, these individuals simply do not feel the words and actions of churches are relevant to their everyday lives or struggles. Many do not feel that religious institutions can be trusted with their vulnerability and pain.

Keeping this in mind, you may find it helpful to reflect on the parable of the Good Samaritan (see Luke 10:29–37) as a model for approaching the season of Lent when it comes to those who are disconnected or alone. In short, many of them are like the victim on the side of the road in Jesus's parable. They are bruised and beaten. They have watched as a devout person and a religious leader passed them by, neglecting to engage them, akin to the reaction of the Levite and the priest (see Luke 10:31–32). How many Ash Wednesdays and Lents have they experienced without the support and kindness of people and leaders of faith? What is needed in Lent is a pastoral approach, the act of a Good Samaritan who, at the sight of the wounded traveler, "went to him and bandaged his wounds…and took care of him" (Luke 10:34). Before we can truly engage a newcomer in an event or a special Lenten initiative, we must tend their wounds, care for them, and accompany them. This can certainly happen in the context of one of those programs, but there should be strong intentionality to offer pastoral care and support. We do not yet know the stories of the people we will encounter on the road, but we should always be mindful that they each have a story filled with joy and struggle and everything in between. Furthermore, we must earn the trust of others, which will be possible only when we spend time with them and invest in their lives and stories. Trust is key if we hope to move forward.

The suggestions that follow are creative ways to offer pastoral care, in particular with those who may be new, those who are skeptical or uncertain, those who were previously disaffiliated or disconnected from religious institutions, and those who were encouraged by members of a welcoming Christian community to continue their journeys of faith beyond Ash Wednesday. While most churches have many already-tested Lenten activities ideal for the active churchgoer wanting to go deeper, these ideas are developed specifically with an outsider in mind and can be adapted to the traditions or customs of many Christian denominations. Underpinning all of them is an opportunity for the community to intentionally engage the stranger, the newcomer, and those who are struggling by forty days of dynamic pastoral accompaniment.

- **Individually reach out.** Using the visitor cards from Ash Wednesday, active churchgoers and leaders can follow up individually (email, text, or phone call) with each person who attended services. This should be done within the first five to ten days of Lent and should be individually directed (not a mass email or text message), so it will require the participation of many active churchgoers, as it will involve more contact than a pastor or church staff could or should handle. Provide talking points for people to use in the invitation process, but make sure the guest who receives the email, text, or phone call does not feel the invitation is taken directly from a script. In this effort, here are some recommendations:

- Express joy and gratitude for the guest's participation on Ash Wednesday; however, do not make it seem like they are being singled out for their absence otherwise.
- Introduce yourself and your own connection to the church (i.e., a parishioner for ten years, serving on the parish staff, a teacher for elementary school children, etc.), but, most important, share a story or a detail about your life beyond the church (i.e., favorite sports team, where you were born and raised, alumni of a local school, etc.).
- If possible, include any specific details of the Ash Wednesday or other recent encounter, to make it as personal as possible.
- Invite the guest to share a little bit about themselves, as they are comfortable.
- Ask if there is anything for which you can pray or offer support.
- Close with an invitation to keep in touch, but do not feel the need to invite them to come to something else at the church (especially if it is

awkward) as the purpose of this outreach is to make contact and establish trust.

- **Write a letter or postcard.** In addition to emails, texts, or phone calls, the act of personally writing a letter or postcard to guests who came on Ash Wednesday will go a long way. This written communication can be done in combination with other forms of outreach. This can be a follow-up to that conversation or just a kind note. The card or letter may have information about the parish, its weekly services or Masses, and Lenten activities, but this should be positioned as an addendum rather than the purpose of the communication. Physically writing something out (more than just a signature) will also show that a person active within the faith community took time for them.

- **Connect with those who recently moved.** When we geographically move into a new town or city, we can feel lost or alone. Our previous network of friends or family now are more removed. Make a concerted effort to reach out to new neighbors soon after they arrive in the local area as a great pastoral outreach at any time, but especially during the Lenten season. Work with your local realtors or find lists of individuals and families who have moved into the zip codes around your church. You can also work with Paulist Evangelization Ministries' New Movers program,[3] which can aid you in locating and communicating with those who have recently moved into your area.

- **Create a sense of belonging.** This is a broad suggestion and individual communities will develop this feeling in a way that seems natural and fitting to their circumstances. The idea is to make every visitor or guest feel as if they already belong to the community. Prior to Lent, assess how people go about becoming a member and even more how people can get actively involved in church ministries or programs to see if it feels more like a gauntlet or a pastoral invitation of love. Getting connected should never feel like a chore but rather an easy movement toward genuine community. During Lent, make every guest feel as though they belong, that they are not strangers.

- **Connect people to counseling services and support groups.** During Lent, make concerted efforts to communicate the opportunities for counseling and connecting them to any support groups that may exist at the church or in the local area. If your congregation does not have these services available, consider starting them. Support groups may include networks for job loss, addiction, divorce, relationship brokenness, mental health issues, new residents to the neighborhood, parents, teens, or those with common interests or experiences.

- **Hold Lenten listening sessions.** One of the reasons some people detach from religious groups is that they do not feel heard by church leaders. On several occasions throughout Lent, hold small-group listening sessions where you take the time to listen to the concerns, questions, doubts, and complaints from the community, most especially from those who are not as active in their religious practice. Hear what they have to say with an open heart, consider their recommendations, let them know that you genuinely care what they have to say, and, most important, follow up with them to share how their suggestions or ideas are being studied or implemented.

- **Encourage guests to share their meatless recipes.** Throughout Lent, invite individuals to bring their homemade meatless dish to the church on Fridays or Sundays. Giving people a chance to contribute something from their family, culture, or inventiveness is a great way to show them that their contribution is vitally important to the overall community. A variation on this idea is asking them to simply share the recipe with the parish and post it in the bulletin or on the website and social media.

- **Invite newcomers to Friday dinners at church.** Abstaining from meat on Fridays is the most observed Lenten ritual. Pair this devotional practice with an experience of community by inviting guests and visitors to a fish fry, spaghetti dinner, or other meatless meal at the church or community center. This invitation can be extended on Ash Wednesday and in subsequent Lenten communications. When hosting those meatless meals at the church, graciously greet and welcome guests and visitors with the highest regard, rather than looking at the fish fry or spaghetti dinner as an event for regular churchgoers. Encourage all active members of your parish to extend great hospitality in whatever ways possible and make guests and visitors feel that they truly belong to your community.

- **Have fun.** While Lent is a penitential season, it does not mean that joy and laughter cannot be part of those forty days. Provide opportunities for social gatherings and experiences, and kindly offer invitations to newcomers. These can include spring and summer sports leagues, group outings to local restaurants or entertainment venues, or potluck dinners at the church or community center. Be especially mindful of the newcomer in promoting or hosting these activities, so they never feel like an outsider crashing the party of an established community.

- **Coordinate a mentorship initiative.** Work with active churchgoers to be part of a mentorship program for newcomers, especially young adults. Ask people already engaged in the community to serve as mentors in their field of work, hobbies or pastimes, neighborhoods, or spiritual matters. Host a training or orientation about what it means to be a mentor.[4] On Ash Wednesday or Sundays during Lent, invite newcomers or guests to consider being part of a mentorship initiative based on their work, interests, local areas, and/ or spiritual growth. Then, pair participants with appropriate mentors. Establish an initial time frame (i.e., the Lenten or Easter season), so the commitment need only be minimal at first. The pair may decide to continue beyond the initial component of the initiative. The mentorship that happens in these settings can be a great pastoral support for those who need a listening ear, sage advice, or the company of another human being who shares their experiences, values, and faith.

LENTEN FRIDAYS

There is something about fish, fasting, and Fridays that has captured the spiritual and religious imagination of people for generations. For centuries, the Church mandated that all adherents over the age of fourteen (and without health restrictions) abstain from meat[5] every Friday of the year, in respect to the day of the week on which Jesus was crucified. After the Second Vatican Council in the 1960s, the Roman Catholic Church allowed each episcopal conference to "determine more precisely the observance of fast and abstinence"[6] within their country. In the United States, the Catholic bishops preserved the Friday tradition in Lent but lifted the dietary obligation for the rest of the year.[7] Today, the Friday fast is still as strong as ever, with six in ten Catholics saying they abstain from meat on Lenten Fridays.[8] Even though these practices are not mandated by other traditions, there are many Christian communities and individuals who choose to fast or abstain from meat on Fridays. It should be pointed out that the words *fasting* and *abstinence* are often used interchangeably, especially regarding regulations around food. While similar, they are actually two distinct concepts. Fasting often refers to limiting one's activity or food for a time, such as the reduction in food consumed on a given day or season (like the number of meals on Ash Wednesday or limiting one's screen time for Lent), while abstinence refers to refraining from one particular activity or food (such as no meat on Fridays).

Regardless of the specific Christian practice or mandate, the centuries-old tradition seems as firmly entrenched in the popular culture as it is in religious circles. In 1962, McDonald's added the Filet-O-Fish sandwich to its menu after Cincinnati franchise owner Lou Groen noticed that his hamburger sales dropped on Fridays due the 87-percent Catholic population in his area. McDonald's corporate founder Ray Kroc agreed, and the item was added to all franchise menus and remains to this day.[9] Sales are especially high in Lent.[10] Likewise, seafood specials and clam chowder as the soup-of-the-day on Fridays are commonplace on the menus at many restaurants and eateries. For centuries, "the day on which Christ died has always been shrouded in sorrow and penance" with a "reputation as the unluckiest day of the week" (for instance, the superstition around Friday the thirteenth).[11] Friday can carry with it the burden of work coupled with the excitement of a forthcoming weekend. The expression "Thank God it's Friday" (and its acronym, TGIF), not to mention a popular restaurant chain using that same sentiment, cements this day in our cultural imagination. This weekly moment of transition, relief, and uncertainty is rooted in the Christian experience, and the long-standing traditions of this day still matter to many people. These stories are but a few examples illustrating the power of Friday spirituality, even beyond the church walls. As already noted, there are strong connections to the Friday fast even for those who do not regularly engage in church activities. As the Pew Research Center discovered, "About six in ten Catholics of all generations abstain from meat on Fridays"—which includes over 40 percent of those who attend church only a few times a year.[12] Throughout this chapter, scattered among the points, there are a few ideas to consider for enriching the already-existing Friday practices of

Christians. Make the most of your Lenten Fridays, as they are also wonderful opportunities to build a bridge to those who are less active in the church.

THE SPIRITUAL PATHWAY

In Lent, the Church emphasizes the personal and communal journey with Jesus. The life of Christ is played out in the Gospel readings during this season. On the First Sunday of Lent, we often hear about Jesus being tempted in the wilderness for forty days. As the weeks progress, we follow the Lord (depending on the specific cycle of readings read during the season) through Jesus's transfiguration, his encounter with the woman at the well, his miracles, the raising of Lazarus from the dead, his nighttime meeting with Nicodemus, and the cleansing of and teaching in the temple. The last week of Lent annually presents the most dramatic moments of Christ's earthly life—his Palm Sunday entrance into Jerusalem, the betrayal of Judas for thirty pieces of silver, the Last Supper, the agony in the Garden of Gethsemane, and Jesus's arrest, trial, beating, crucifixion, and burial on Good Friday. The totality of the season offers a quick narrative of Christ's human journey. It is not that Christians and church leaders forget Jesus the rest of the year; however, during Lent, the events of his earthly life are presented in rapid succession, relatively speaking. The fact that the length of our forty-day sojourn is based on Jesus's own forty-day experience in the desert further cements this point. We emulate the acts of the Lord during this time by fasting just as he did, though our Lenten sacrifices may not be nearly as intense as what Jesus would have done during that time. Nonetheless, we are following in Jesus's footsteps during Lent. The intimate connection to the experience of Jesus may appeal to people on the margins of church engagement, who consider themselves spiritual but not religious. Among these individuals, many find solace in Christ but not as much in Christian churches.

It is important to approach Lenten practices with these people in mind. At minimum, it is worth considering offering a variety of initiatives for this annual season for people on various points along the spiritual path. As much as possible, in whatever spiritual offerings your church provides during Lent, make sure it is apparent and explicit *who* is at the core of your efforts: Jesus. Let those who are not normally active in religious activities know that your efforts are centered in Christ. This may be done in your external communications and in the personal invitations that are offered on Ash Wednesday and during Lent. Furthermore, it is important to evaluate *the way* in which you are communicating your spiritual messages and activities, particularly as it may be received by those who are not closely involved in your community. Before sending out any promotion about spiritual activities, consider how it may be received by someone who is not familiar with your tradition's religious or spiritual jargon, customs, or history. Review how a religiously inactive person might understand that communication. This may mean reframing religious rituals or programs in spiritual or secular language, so that those who are not religious might better understand and appreciate it. You may also notice these alternative communication phrases or words used throughout the rest of this book. Here are a few suggestions on ways to look anew at Lenten spiritual activities through the lens of a newcomer, guest, or someone unfamiliar with or with a suspicious eye toward religious institutions.

- **Give out spiritual guides and calendars.** Before Lent, develop a small guidebook for Lent with an eye toward guests and visitors. This booklet can include Lenten prayers or some specific prayers for or about your local community as well as a calendar for the season. Within this calendar, you can offer simple, daily ideas for how one can honor each day of Lent, as well as notes about upcoming opportunities within your church that take place during these forty days. These booklets can be given out the weekend(s) before Lent, on Ash Wednesday, and throughout Lent. Make sure that there are enough copies (or an online edition exists) so that visitors get these booklets first.

- **Pray for forty people.** Encourage both newcomers and regular churchgoers to take on a forty-day challenge of praying for forty different individuals on each day of Lent. These forty intentions can be for either a collection of people known to the individual or other members of the congregation or local community. This daily discipline may be a great way to guide one's prayer life from inward to outward focused. As Katie, a young adult Catholic from Indianapolis, notes, "By far my favorite Lent was when I decided to pray for a different person, in detail, every day for forty days....It was a great exercise in paying attention."[13]

- **Offer a Lenten tour.** On Friday evenings, weekend mornings, after services or Masses, or at publicized occasions during Lent, give short tours of your worship space. Provide details about the sanctuary and the building(s) from their history to the meanings behind various components and/or artwork. Most important, though, share some of your own personal stories of the space and what makes this place special to you. Providing tours can help guests feel more comfortable and understanding of a site that is sacred and special to you and your congregation.

- **Teach about your liturgy.** If you are part of a liturgical Christian tradition, use Lent as an opportunity to teach about the rituals associated with regular worship. During Lent, hold teaching liturgies to explain the background of your rituals. Be sure to include your own experiences of liturgy and why it is personally meaningful for you. Offering this program can also help newcomers feel more comfortable with worship, which may prompt them to consider coming back in the future.

- **Host Lenten mornings or evenings for "stress relief."** People need rest and refuge, and during Lent, you can open your church for moments of peace and calm. No complex programming is necessary, though church staff or community leaders may want to be on hand for pastoral support. Consider using candlelight or low lighting, creating an environment that lends itself to spiritual rest. Within these moments, offer simple, uncomplicated experiences of prayer and spirituality from within your Christian tradition that convey peace and calm for a weary world, such as candlelight and silence, centering prayer, meditation, Taizé, rosary, eucharistic adoration, Liturgy of the Hours, Stations of the Cross, a labyrinth, or *lectio divina*, among others. Whatever form is used, make sure that it is conducted in a manner that respects a visitor's need for relieving anxiety and finding holy peace. Provide prayer aids for those who may be seeking guidance on how best to use this moment of refuge. In addition, in communications and invitations, it may be best to use nonreligious terms or phrases like *stress relief* or *unpacking your burdens* rather than insider language. This is also important because many individuals enter the season with stress, burdens, and past mistakes that weigh on them. Ash Wednesday may be a start toward reconciliation, but only so much can be done within one liturgy. It may be helpful to further complement these quiet experiences with accompaniment offerings from within your religious tradition, congregation, or community like pastoral counseling, spiritual direction or companionship, support group meetings, communal reconciliation services, or the sacrament of reconciliation.

- **Host a "busy person's" retreat.** Like active churchgoers, there are many disaffiliated people longing for a chance to rest or find silence amid their noisy lives; however, like so many of us, they find it hard to carve out the necessary time for such an experience. With these people in mind, offer a "busy person's" retreat. These experiences can take place in short segments during Lent. A person can be individually directed by church leaders through regular prayer experiences, spiritual direction or companionship, and participation in occasional group gatherings (at the church or at someone's home) with others in the area who are going through a similar "busy person's" journey.

- **Think of small groups in new ways.** When planning Lenten small groups, keep in mind potential

newcomers who may be introverts or uncomfortable with sharing their personal stories or faith
experiences with others, or who may be unfamiliar with Scripture. Consider hosting a small
group in an online setting (on social media, for
instance) and having facilitators in those small
groups look out for discomfort or fear among
guests. You may even plan on making the groups
even smaller to allow for easing into these experiences.

- **Go the distance.** Coordinate small pilgrim-
ages or trips to sacred places, shrines, or other
churches in Lent. The physical experience of
journeying together to these sites can be appealing to guests who may be curious about what
makes places spiritually important. It also gives
people a chance to see new things and allows for
comradery with others on the trip across town
or region. In a sense, by visiting another sacred
site, regular churchgoers and newcomers are
both "pilgrim visitors" in a new place together,
creating a greater sense of solidarity and familiarity between them.

- **Take people "back in time."** With its focus on
personal introspection on our past, and the key
moments in the life of Jesus of Nazareth two
thousand years ago, Lent allows us to go "back in
time." Take advantage of this openness to the past
by providing opportunities for regular churchgoers and Lenten visitors to learn more about Jesus,
the history of the season, and the Christian story
in general. Frame the offerings as a chance to go
"back in time" and have fun with a time traveler's
look at the story of faith. Another creative way

of doing this is hosting movie nights at home or at the church (with proper permissions and respecting copyright law, of course), along with discussions on the spirituality of biblical, Christian, or other movies with spiritual themes. This may be a less threatening way to get new or less active churchgoers to open up about Jesus, the Scriptures, or the Christian faith. And be sure to have good popcorn and snacks on hand for this potentially lively and thought-provoking dialogue.

- **Hold Friday prayer experiences in local communities.** When planning Lenten prayer experiences, consider gathering in a setting outside the church grounds: in a community center, library, park, town square, school or university campus, shopping area, or neighborhood. These settings may be more inviting to those who are less active or comfortable in churches or religious institutions. You can also gather in people's homes if your community is open to this. Small faith-sharing groups, Bible studies, prayer services, social gatherings or meals, and the like can be successful in intimate, home-based settings. This idea emulates Jesus in the story of Zacchaeus (see Luke 19:1–10) by asking a newcomer if they might consider hosting a Lenten program in their own home. Give a guest or returning churchgoer an opportunity to serve as host for others in their community. Of course, these ideas are unconventional and may be a logistical challenge in various circumstances (and may require additional safeguards); however, just considering these radical directions can stretch us beyond our comfort zone.

STATIONS OF THE CROSS

Throughout Lent, especially on Fridays, many mainline Christian traditions around the world hold Stations of the Cross (or Way of the Cross) services, marking points along the *Via Dolorosa* (Road of Sorrows) of Jesus on his way to crucifixion, an ancient prayer experience practiced for centuries and within many cultures. Because of its long-lasting place in the Christian experience, the relative familiarity with it can make it an ideal experience for Lenten visitors and guests. The Stations are, for the most part, a brief and straight-forward prayer service. The simplicity of reflecting and praying through the passion and death of Jesus makes the ritual accessible to many people. With few exceptions, these services are not overly complicated, and churches can provide easy-to-follow prayer guides.

This ritual may be prayed individually; however, a communal experience of this service can be very powerful. Praying or walking alongside others is vivid; it is a visual reminder that Jesus walks with all of us and that his death means salvation for everyone. Furthermore, the collective experience can strengthen a sense of belonging. Some suggestions to consider include:

Ask guests to take the lead roles. When praying the Stations of the Cross, invite newcomers or guests to take a leading role. Ask them to read, carry a processional cross, lead a song, or take another responsibility. The very act of asking them to step forward as a leader, no matter how small or simple the task might be, could be incredibly significant for their self-worth and sense of belonging. And be okay if they decline the offer and extend a note of gratitude for considering the request.

Focus the Stations of the Cross around newcomers' concerns. Consider the issues that newcomers and disaffiliated individuals are dealing with in their lives: uncertainty, economic worries, health issues, personal brokenness, anxiety, and stress, to name a few. Incorporate some or all of these concerns in the prayers of the Stations of the Cross service or invite people to share their personal concerns after each station, to unite their struggles with those of Jesus under the weight of the cross.

Allow for sacred silence and contemplation. In some instances, the Stations of the Cross service can be a very brief prayer experience; however, resist the urge to conclude quickly. Provide time for extended moments of silence. Explain in advance why you are pausing. Invite participants to use the silence to slow down from the anxieties of the week and rest in the Lord during contemplative silence.

Gather socially before or after Stations of the Cross. Adjacent to the prayer service, create a sense of community and belonging by gathering for a meal or a social outing. Out of respect for Friday fasting and simplicity, the occasion should not be extravagant and should have limited food options for those observing Friday abstinence. If done afterward, select a meeting place that can grow the relationships of participants while providing them with a number of meatless or simple food options.

THE DOMESTIC AND DIGITAL CHURCH

Most people experience the season of Lent outside the church walls. Fasting, abstaining from meat, giving to charities, and private prayer are the traditional components of Lent, but they do not require being in a church to do them. The Gospel reading for Ash Wednesday (Matt 6:1–6, 16–18) even encourages these private acts of personal devotion. Furthermore, acts of individual spirituality are commonplace, even among those who do not attend church regularly. Silent prayer, Bible reading, fasting, donating to charities, and engaging in social justice are, to varying degrees, popular among Americans who otherwise avoid religion, and most are done in the privacy of one's home. This does not mean that church leaders cannot have an impact on the lives of those who engage in these spiritual practices, especially during the season of Lent. It is important for active churchgoers to be mindful that people are open to sustaining a spiritual life and that this inclination may be fulfilled through private traditions and digital engagement around matters of faith. Each situation is unique, and interpersonal relationships are complex. It is hard to advise churchgoers what to do in their homes or online because the best course of action will largely depend on the history, nuances, and sensitivities of each family. Being aware of these particulars, though, can help you navigate how to proceed in domestic and digital settings.

Nonetheless, what follows are suggestions for tapping into the spiritual life of Lenten visitors at home and online. They can work for some situations but not others, so before jumping in, discern carefully what might work best for the realities of the relationships in question. These are ideas that can be done by church leaders in their own domestic and digital lives, as well as suggestions that can be offered to active churchgoers within their congregations.

- **Listen around the dinner table.** Whether you live in an intergenerational household or friends or family come for a meal, take time to listen to the realities and struggles those loved ones are experiencing. Rather than trying to figure out how to get a person back to church, pause for a moment to simply listen to and be moved by the struggles they are facing. These difficulties may be *eclipsing* their lives, preventing them from connecting with religious institutions or a community of faith.[14] In these cases, it is best not to try to fix the situation but to listen with tender compassion.

- **Ask questions.** Spark conversation at the dinner table or over the phone with a family member or friend who is less active in the practice of faith by asking questions such as the following: What was your Ash Wednesday experience like this year? or What are you giving up for Lent? You may want to reminisce about your shared memories of past Lents together (especially if there is a family connection). Share your own stories and plans, and do not offer critique or judgment of the other person's responses.

- **Encourage personal spirituality.** If friends and family share something regarding their spirituality (i.e., talking to God, reading Bible verses, etc.), no matter how seemingly insignificant it may be to you, affirm and encourage the gestures. In addition, ask deeper questions about those spiritual moments, but do not push others too strongly to the next level (i.e., going to church every Sunday, joining a parish). It is more important to acknowledge those occasions and authentically celebrate them.

- **Share your personal devotions.** Rather than trying to convince a friend or family member to engage in your own favorite or meaningful devotion (i.e., going to Sunday worship, fasting, family traditions, particular acts of prayer, meditation), simply share how those experiences have been helpful to you through the years. Be vulnerable with that person in sharing your Lenten routines and how they have helped you. When an individual sees why and how a certain devotion is special or life-giving to someone they love, it could break down barriers. At that point, it is not necessary to invite or encourage them to partake in the same act. Just share your story.

- **Put peanut butter and jelly in the kitchen cabinet on Fridays.** It may seem like an overly simple measure but intentionally placing meatless items in your refrigerator or kitchen cabinet helps encourage and maintain the Lenten Friday fast within the family. Consider also making a point of eating the last of your meat dishes each

Thursday night in Lent in a weekly mini Mardi Gras–like tradition, to remind others in your household that Friday is a special occasion for fasting. The Thursday ritual could also be a way of bonding the family together throughout Lent.

- **Send weekly Lenten communications.** With the contact information collected on Ash Wednesday or through other means, church leaders can send out weekly emails or texts. The communication should not primarily be a marketing solicitation, though an invitation to upcoming activities can be included. Rather, it should primarily provide prayer, service, or charity opportunities, and Lenten inspiration.

- **Host a digital Lenten retreat.** Consider offering a Lenten online retreat. This option is especially good for people who cannot commit to a regular night or an entire weekend for a retreat-like experience. This may be done by posting Lenten inspiration and challenges every few days on a special webpage (either on the church website or elsewhere) from Ash Wednesday through Holy Week. Alternatively, you can dedicate a specific week for posting daily content, inviting feedback at the times most convenient for participants, and perhaps having a few livestreamed events within that timeframe. There are also many organizations and individuals that already offer online Lenten retreats, and churches can go through one together in small groups; this option may also be helpful for busy church leaders who may not have time to coordinate an online experience of their own, and good online retreat options do exist.

- **Talk about positive digital fasting**. A growing number of people give up their social media access for Lent, especially if they have grown too attached to their mobile devices or certain apps. This is certainly an admirable exercise. Consider inviting individuals who do not give up social media for Lent to also fast from the gossip or mindless scrolling online. Suggest that they make social media usage more positive or meaningful by spending time praying over and making deeper connections with their digital connections, especially those who need their love and support, or with a person who has been distant or less communicative in recent years.

A SOCIALLY JUST LENT

Many people today want to be more involved in society and change the world for the better. In a recent multiyear listening process done with young people, a network of ministry leaders repeatedly found "the desire of youth and young adults to make a difference in the world through service to those in need."[15] It echoes what Catholic bishops found in their own global analysis a few years earlier: "Albeit in a different way from earlier generations, social commitment is a specific feature of today's young people. Alongside some who are indifferent, there are many others who are ready to commit themselves to initiatives of voluntary work, active citizenship, and social solidarity."[16]

This inclination to service and social change is also evident across older generations. Despite the reputation that young people are most prone to political and civic engagement, data has shown that all age groups are equally engaged

129

in service work and volunteerism.[17] Over a quarter of all adults in the United States volunteer annually, and religious organizations are the source of approximately one-third of that engagement.[18] These statistics indicate that there is a desire for social action among all generations.

With its emphasis on almsgiving and charity, the precepts of the Lenten season align well with the secular attention given to active engagement with social causes and concerns. Some of those who are less religiously active are still invested in volunteerism, justice activism, and charitable giving. Some individuals may express their connection to a higher power through their social actions on behalf of those who are poor, suffering, marginalized, or victimized. Anna, a young adult from Seattle, notes that the Lenten connection to justice keeps her motivated in her faith. She says that Lent "means sometimes I'm actively giving up things [and] sometimes the things I 'give up' are of my time in order to take on a commitment to something else: daily actions for political advocacy on a topic and a commitment to service."[19]

Local churches can build on this desire by emphasizing almsgiving and social action on behalf of the people on the peripheries during Lent. This emphasis may better engage guests, newcomers, and those less active in religious institutions. It is not, by any means, a stretch for church leaders to make these connections, as the Lenten season is a great time to align one's poverty of spirit with the physical poverty and hardship of other human beings. Here are some suggestions for looking anew at a church's social and charitable works during Lent through the lens of the visitor or newcomer:

- **More intentionally emphasize Lenten almsgiving**. Among the core pillars of Lent, prayer and fasting are usually encouraged within Christian communities; however, almsgiving or charity may be less emphasized. Because these aspects of our Lenten tradition are often appealing to youth, young adults, and many others, consider highlighting your church's work with social justice and service. Talk about these elements during Ash Wednesday and Sunday worship in Lent and through your church communications. With so many Christian communities honoring the season of Lent, this time of year could also be an opportunity to collaborate ecumenically with nearby churches in organizing service and justice projects, with an emphasis toward engaging newcomers, visitors, and young adults within each of those Christian churches.

- **Invite people to be more active in social justice.** When considering the opportunities to which we can invite Lenten visitors and guests, make a concerted effort to encourage a sense of social responsibility and action on the part of active churchgoers. Encourage parishioners and members to learn more about the gospel call to justice, to volunteer with those most in need, and to get involved with community advocacy and engaging with the community's work in social justice.

- **Amplify the work of national charities.** During Lent, the work of national and global charities (such as Catholic Relief Services, Lutheran World Relief, Lutheran Services in America, World Vision, the Salvation Army, Catholic Charities, Compassion International, the Catholic Campaign for Human Development, among many others) are excellent ways to encourage a more global spirit of almsgiving. Connecting to these organizations can also raise their awareness of the ecumenical and international solidarity of Lent and provide a chance for people to engage beyond the local area.

- **Encourage daily Lenten giving.** Since many are attracted to the simple commitments of Lent, encourage daily exercises in almsgiving. One nationwide program that provides a great tool is the Catholic Relief Services (CRS) Rice Bowl initiative, which gives individuals a chance to put spare change and small donations toward humanitarian aid each day or at any moment. Originally intended for children, this initiative can be a simple guide for any adult, especially guests and visitors.

- **Ask newcomers to volunteer in the community.** When newcomers arrive on Ash Wednesday, consider ways to invite them to volunteer their time and energy for specific social projects or activities within the local area. These may include volunteering at soup kitchens, shelters, thrift stores, donation centers, environmental clean-up efforts, nursing homes, community centers, correction facilities, or other places in need of volunteers and support. This work can give people excellent ways to live out Lenten almsgiving. In addition to short-term efforts, Lent can also be a time when people may want to consider long-lasting volunteerism through ongoing relationships with nearby charities or service organizations. This may include connecting with nationwide volunteerism efforts, such as Ameri-Corps, Jesuit Volunteer Corps, the Catholic Volunteer Network, the National Park Service, the Knights of Columbus, Shriners Hospital for Children, and many others.

- **Host a Lenten service/justice speaker series.** To get newcomers excited about the prospect of making a difference in their community or the world, bring in speakers who are active in service and social justice. During the weeks of Lent, host regular gatherings where these talks can be featured.
- **Hold a forty-hour fast for poverty awareness.** In honor of the number forty, so integral to the Lenten journey, consider hosting a forty-hour (two-day) exercise in fasting (i.e., no major meals, no meat, or no food between sunrise and sunset, or in a manner fitting to your community). This can be done in a retreat-type setting over a weekend or at any point in the week done on your own at home. The purpose of the fast would be to raise awareness of hunger and poverty in the area and around the world. With that in mind, during this fast, participants can learn more about antipoverty initiatives and charities or take part in acts of service or justice.
- **Engage in a local ecology mission for Lent.** The Lenten season aligns with the warming springtime in northern climates, which allows for some outdoor activity. Get people involved with an ecology mission doing park or nature preserve clean-up; connecting with the environmental sustainability measures in the county, state, or nation; or learning more about the Christian connections to ecological justice.
- **Lead Lenten justice marches, advocacy efforts, and protests.** Another form of almsgiving that

may be practiced in Lent is advocacy work: marches for various causes, protests for justice, and communicating to and working with elected officials on behalf of the poor and marginalized. Churches can coordinate these within their area and be intentional about inviting new people into this work, especially those who share that they have a heart for certain issues of social justice.

- **Eat local on Fridays.** Encourage regular church-goers and newcomers to support the neighbor-hood economy by intentionally patronizing local establishments (with meatless options) on Fridays. Doing this can build consciousness and develop habits of helping one's neighbors in their service to the community, while bringing atten-tion to the spiritual draw of Lenten Fridays. This measure can also teach participants about local sustainable growth and dignity of the worker.

- **Invite and form newcomers for community leadership.** It may seem counterintuitive to think about bringing a person new to the com-munity during Lent into a leadership role, but this is a radical measure of hospitality to trust guests with key responsibilities in the congrega-tion. Think about potential ways to invite them into a leadership role if the person seems willing to connect further. Allow their wisdom to have an influence on you and your church and men-tor them as best you can. Be sure to accompany and support them through the initial experi-ence should their initial enthusiasm wane in the weeks or months following a positive moment of encounter.

INSPIRED BY THE STAGE AND SCREEN

When I was younger, I became truly fascinated with the Lenten story, especially the drama of Jesus's final week. This was further enhanced by my own love of cinematic spectacle from an early age. Our family's movie collection included not only all of George Lucas's original *Star Wars* trilogy (1977–83) and Steven Spielberg's first three *Indiana Jones* movies (1981–89), but also William Wyler's Oscar-winning masterpiece, *Ben-Hur* (1959) with Charlton Heston, and Nicholas Ray's classic film, *King of Kings* (1961) with Jeffrey Hunter, as well as the film adaptation of Andrew Lloyd Weber's 1970 rock opera, *Jesus Christ Superstar* (1973), and Franco Zeffirelli's beloved television miniseries, *Jesus of Nazareth* (1977). Those movies were part of my own Lenten journey each year and my growing understanding of God, as the intensity of the life of Christ played out in dramatic fashion before my eyes. They caught my attention at a young age, and, to this day, their sights and sounds are what play out in my mind every time I hear the Lenten readings and the Holy Week passion narrative. I was so captivated by these accounts that, as a high school freshman, I asked my pastor if I could organize a student passion play so that, during Holy Week, the young people of our parish could tell Jesus's story to the rest of the community in a dramatic and engaging way. Looking back on that experience, perhaps I wanted to enter the story myself, to physically walk side by side with the Lord. Each year that followed, our passion play project attracted more participants, including several young people who had little interest in the church but were personally invited by their friends to get involved. When I left for college, I brought the passion play with me, encouraging my fraternity brothers and students from Lutheran, Catholic, Methodist, and even agnostic backgrounds to take part. After several grueling weeks of rehearsals throughout Lent, we hosted performances for large crowds on campus and in the local community during Holy Week. There was something about literally immersing oneself in the drama of the Lord's story that drew people in. These formative Lenten moments, along with the shared experiences with my peers in high school and in college, solidified my own faith journey for years to come.

THE DRAMA OF HOLY WEEK

Each year, Holy Week presents a dramatic story to follow. The liturgies, prayers, and commemorations of the days from Palm Sunday to Easter Sunday clearly exhibit the intensity of Jesus's final week before his death and resurrection. Human beings are drawn to drama and story. The biblical account of Christ's passion is an incredible narrative that draws in so many people. When American author Fulton Oursler wrote his 1949 book about the life of Jesus, he affirmed this understanding by titling it *The Greatest Story Ever Told*. The book was made into a movie by the same name in 1965.

The fact that Jesus's dramatic story is the culmination of Lent is why many may feel compelled to engage it further. Parishes and congregations can enhance their Holy Week efforts by intentionally considering how newcomers, guests, visitors, and those who do not frequent church will perceive these movements. Just as it was recommended to emphasize Jesus's humanity in Lent, it is just as important to accentuate Jesus's incredible story during Holy Week. Communicate the drama, movement, and emotional journey of this moment, and in so doing, invite others more deeply into the breathtaking narrative of Lent's final days.

Here are some suggestions for making those Holy Week connections:

- **Invite guests into the drama.** One radical way to welcome visitors is to invite them to take part in a dramatization of the last days or hours of Jesus through an organized passion play (see sidebar, "My Lenten Journey"); in the liturgy of Palm Sunday, Holy Thursday, or Good Friday; or in a special Easter choir. In some churches, this might also include a tradition of hosting a "living" Stations of the Cross (i.e., enacting or watching others act out, or create a human tableau of, the fourteen Stations rather than viewing images of the Stations on the church walls). It may require varying levels of set-up and preparation, but drama experiences can have great impact for all involved. Having guests literally walk beside the Lord can be a powerful moment, as can the weekly rehearsals that foster community among participants. The resulting drama can be held during Holy Week so that Lent can be spent practicing, praying, and connecting.
- **Make Palm Sunday more than the palms.** Palm Sunday is often one of the most well-attended days of the church year, as it inaugurates the drama of Holy Week. In many communities, that drama literally plays out on the altar as the long Gospel reading of the Lord's passion is often conveyed with different speakers reading the lines of Jesus, Pilate, and the disciples and the congregation serving as "the crowd." In planning

Palm Sunday, think of ways to involve Lenten visitors: encouraging them to wear something red (the traditional color of the feast), including them in a walking procession of palms, and inviting them to read one of the parts of the Gospel.

- **Capture attention on Spy Wednesday.** The traditional Gospel reading for the Wednesday of Holy Week focuses on the story of Judas Iscariot (see Matt 26:14–25), who received thirty pieces of silver for giving over Jesus to the high priests and "from that moment he began to look for an opportunity to betray him" (Matt 26:16). Because this is the moment when Judas became a *spy* for the authorities, this day of the week became known as *Spy Wednesday*, a rather unique and memorable moniker. Because of its fascinating sound, it could be an opportunity to capture the attention of less active Christians for some programs around the themes of betrayal, duplicity, or desperation, which may be of interest to them as they make their way through Holy Week.

- **Move hearts with Tenebrae.** The ritual ceremony of Tenebrae may be an ideal opportunity for people who are seeking a feeling of transcendence or spiritual illumination during the last week of Lent. This prayer experience involves a reading of Scripture, especially the Psalms, punctuated throughout by a gradual extinguishing of candles. It concludes with a sudden loud noise done in total darkness. The ancient and majestic rite is often held on the middle or latter half of Holy Week (depending on the Christian tradition), though not exclusively. Making a personal invitation or promotion of it, with a simple explanation, is highly recommended.

- **Participate in a Seder meal.** If possible, work with a local Jewish community or family to participate in a Seder meal, which was the type of supper that Jesus would have eaten with his disciples on the night before his crucifixion, rooted in the Passover story. Inviting newcomers to this sacred rite can be a wonderful opportunity for interreligious dialogue and having a better understanding of the religious traditions of Jesus and his disciples. NOTE: Out of respect to the Jewish community and the integrity of the ritual, it is *not* recommended that this act be done by Christians as a reenactment of the Last Supper or to "baptize" it by concluding its celebration with a Gospel reading or the Eucharist. Allow it to exist in its proper and dignified form.[20] Work with your local synagogue to explore options to do this in the best way possible.

- **Join the Lord in the Upper Room.** Holy (Maundy) Thursday occupies a special place in Christian remembrance: it is the day of the Lord's Supper (cf. Matt 26:17–35; Mark 14:12–31; Luke 22:14–38; John 13–17), when Jesus instituted the Holy Eucharist and gave his final teachings to the apostles. Through your denomination's particular liturgy this day, invite visitors to feel as if they are joining the Lord in the Upper Room through a meaningful, transcendent, and sacred worship experience. Be mindful of the newcomer or less religiously active individual who comes to church on this day, recognizing its importance in their pre-Easter traditions.

- **Wash guests' feet on Holy Thursday.** During the Holy Thursday rite in several traditions, it is also customary to imitate Jesus's act of washing the disciples' feet (see John 13:1–20). If this is a local custom in your community, consider inviting newcomers and guests to have their feet washed (and, furthermore, washed first or by the pastor or congregational leader). This act symbolizes a sense of humility before another person. Imagine the impact it will have for someone who does not attend church as often or is aware of their own insecurities, shortcomings, or mistakes.
- **Embark on a "midnight pilgrimage."** In some Christian traditions, a popular Holy Thursday custom is to make short visits to churches to stop and pray, in imitation of Jesus's request to his disciples in the Garden of Gethsemane, "Remain here, and stay awake with me" (Matt 26:38). These visits take place until the churches close their doors for the evening, usually around midnight. Consider organizing your own "midnight pilgrimage" for your community, either by foot, by a caravan of cars, or by renting a van or bus to transport people from church to church. Those who are new may appreciate the unique custom, the experience of seeing new places, and conversing with other "midnight pilgrims" who can make them feel a sense of belonging along the way.
- **Share the intensity of the Lord's passion.** On Good Friday, it is important to extend personal invitations to newcomers to join you for services during the day or in the evening to mark the

commemoration of the Lord's crucifixion and burial. Be mindful of and offer radical hospitality to guests on this sacred day. Recognize that there are many who may be attending services that day for the first time since Ash Wednesday or since last year. When hosting services, share the spiritual intensity of the moment, which may have additional significance for those needing to align their personal struggles with the sufferings of the Lord on the cross.

- **Advocate for life on Good Friday.** Since there are many disaffiliated individuals drawn to the work of advocacy and justice, offer opportunities for active churchgoers and newcomers to join together in advocating for life on Good Friday, the day on which Jesus's human life was taken from him. Stand or march against the death penalty, abortion, euthanasia, war, or gun violence. In a particular way, since so much attention is drawn to the Jerusalem setting of the crucifixion this day, advocate also for peace in the Holy Land and an eradication of war and the persecution of Jews, Christians, and Muslims in those parts of the world.
- **Host a silent retreat on Holy Saturday.** The time between the Good Friday commemoration and the Easter celebration is a quiet moment on the liturgical calendar. This marks the period when Jesus was in the tomb, so there is a stillness that reigns over people's hearts and minds on Holy Saturday. This could be a perfect opportunity for a morning/daytime silent retreat or an overnight retreat starting in the evening of Good Friday. Invite people to the church, retreat center,

or a sacred space to soak in that stillness, and reflect on the absence of noise and action on that day—something that those overwhelmed with life and busyness might be craving as they journey through Lent. Holy Week and Easter weekend can be very busy times for church staff and parish leadership, so the effort of hosting a retreat in the midst of these sacred days may not be possible. If this is the case for your community, consider preparing well-trained volunteers in advance to lead this retreat experience for others.

- **Bless family Easter baskets**. An Eastern European tradition, which my own Polish family regularly observed, was the blessing of the Easter foods and baskets on Holy Saturday. For families who are not regular churchgoers, this custom may be a creative opportunity to engage them before Easter. The connection to family meals and the sacredness of the food God provides us could be ways to connect those whose personal and familial obligations eclipse their regular religious engagement.

- **Draw newcomers to the Easter Vigil**. The drama of Holy Week reaches its climax on Easter, when the pain and suffering of the Lord's passion are vanquished in the miracle of resurrection. The liturgy, in particular the Easter Vigil rite (common in several Christian traditions), has many elements that tell the entire story of salvation and Jesus's victory over death. Because of its complexity, it may be helpful for regular churchgoers to physically accompany visitors and guests during this service, providing explanations along the way. Alternatively, the church may offer a short guidebook that explains the various movements of the ritual. Seeing the baptism and confirmation of new Christians may be a reminder of their own initiation or early experiences of faith and inspire them to consider deepening their own faith commitment beyond Easter.

- **Celebrate guests on Easter Sunday.** During the Masses or services on Easter Sunday, make a concerted effort to welcome and celebrate the presence of visitors, guests, and newcomers. Using the methods of hospitality carried out on Ash Wednesday (see chapter 4), make those who return for this holy celebration also feel acknowledged and that they belong to your community. Consider ways to offer warm Easter greetings as people arrive and find their seats. As the liturgy is finished, make sure that the active churchgoers are fully attentive and caring to the newcomers in their midst that day.

REFLECT AND EVALUATE

Immediately following Lent and Easter each year, it is important to pause in thanksgiving for the experience. Beginning with Ash Wednesday and throughout the Lenten season, people are having moments of return to faith practices. It is important to spend time individually or as a community to give thanks to God for the presence of these unexpected guests and fellow travelers over the past forty days. It can be easy to simply move on to the next big thing, but taking time in the Easter season to prayerfully acknowledge the joyful reconnections that may have occurred is very good for the soul and for the continued appreciation for the Lord's graces.

It may be helpful for community members to share with one another the encounters they had from the beginning of Lent through Easter with people who were previously unknown to them. It may be as simple as a smile or a brief conversation with a guest in the same pew or as deep as a growing relationship between a parish leader and a newcomer who attended every week. Reflecting on and praying for these beautiful moments is a perfect way to acknowledge the graced encounters that took place along our way. Once this reflection takes place, it is also beneficial to make literal note of these moments by collecting and recording them. In addition, be sure to evaluate and seriously discuss what can be done better in the future. What were occasions when the active churchgoers missed an opportunity to accompany a guest or visitor? When was an activity or event held at the church that was not as welcoming as it should have been? Who or what was missing from this past Lent's journey? What could be improved or developed further if done again the following Lent? Keeping track of those insights and shortcomings, while challenging at first, is a helpful tool to ensure growth for the future.

Chapter 6

BEYOND THE ASHES

And a steadfast spirit renew within me.
(Ps 51:12)

—from the Ash Wednesday Psalm Reading

Beyond Lent, are there other times people will come back to church? What can we take from our experiences on Ash Wednesday and Lent for the rest of the year?

By taking up the challenge of welcoming and accompanying Lenten visitors, we not only ensure a stronger connection for forty days but also rediscover our Christian identity and rootedness—and in so doing, potentially transform our communities of faith year-round. Pope Francis addresses this in his 2013 exhortation, *Evangelii Gaudium*:

> The Church must look more closely and sympathetically at others whenever necessary. In our world, ordained ministers and other pastoral workers can make present the fragrance of Christ's closeness and his personal gaze. The Church will have to initiate everyone...into this "art of accompaniment" which teaches us to remove our sandals before the sacred ground of the other (cf. Exod 3:5). The pace

of this accompaniment must be steady and reassur-
ing, reflecting our closeness and our compassionate gaze which also heals, liberates, and encourages
growth in the Christian life. (§169)[1]

Through our intentional preparation for and encounter
with the newcomers, visitors, guests, and those who reconnect
briefly with Lenten traditions, we learn this "art of accompaniment" because we recognize God present in those who visit
our faith communities. Like Moses before the burning bush,
we can "have the farsightedness to appreciate the little flame
that continues to burn" (*Christus Vivit* 67)[2] in their hearts and
praise God for this opportunity to encounter the divine spark
yet again in the soul of another. When done well, the ministry
we do before and throughout Lent is truly "steady and reas-
suring" and offers to those otherwise disconnected and struggling individuals we encounter "our compassionate gaze" that
"heals, liberates, and encourages growth in the Christian life."
This has been our goal for Lent, but the journey does not end
here. As Pope Francis indicates, engaging in this Lenten "art of
accompaniment" is but a starting point (*Evangelii Gaudium*
169). The journey is far from over once Easter arrives.

Our experience on Ash Wednesday and during Lent
allows us to rediscover what it means to be an intentionally
compassionate, accompanying, and mission-focused Christian community that seeks to heal, liberate, and encourage
growth in others, especially those who are struggling, isolated, and uncertain. On Ash Wednesday, we hear the Psalmist proclaim, "In the greatness of your compassion wipe out
my offense" (Ps 51:3), and, through our Lenten accompaniment, we seek to follow the Lord's compassionate example.
By putting Christ front and center through our love of the
visitor and the stranger, we emulate the greatness of God's
merciful concern through our concrete actions.

Forty days of engaging in this intentional outreach can be exhausting for anyone. While it gives church leaders opportunities to act as Christian ambassadors, it may be challenging to hear the Lord ask us to keep going even further. The Psalmist (Ps 51:12–14, 17) seems to know our reticence as we hear him say:

> A clean heart create for me, O God,
>   and a steadfast spirit renew within me.
> Cast me not out from your presence,
>   and your Holy Spirit take not from me.
> Give me back the joy of your salvation,
>   and a willing spirit sustain in me.
> O Lord, open my lips,
>   and my mouth shall proclaim your praise.

We are challenged by the words "a steadfast spirit renew within me" and "a willing spirit sustain in me" as we look beyond Lent into the rest of the calendar year. God asks us to keep going, to stay alert as missionary disciples, now trained and equipped in this "art of accompaniment" (*Evangelii Gaudium* 169).

Ironically, although Lent is modeled on Jesus's forty-day sojourn into the desert, our greatest temptations often lie beyond that season, when our guard is down. We might wonder if we can finally take a break after six weeks of missionary work. Yet God asks Christians and church leaders to maintain a "steadfast spirit" and continue what we started in his name in Lent for the rest of the year. Beyond the Lenten season, we can find even more opportunities to remain steadfast in this mission. Lent was a great start, but there are other ways to live out our Christian story and really transform our churches and ourselves for the entire year.

BEING PREPARED FOR MORE MOMENTS OF RETURN

While some of the most significant annual moments of return occur on Ash Wednesday and in Lent (and the ones that are most helpful for reconnecting visitors and guests), they are not the only ones. Christmas is, by and large, the most prominent time when individuals return to communal worship, and there are other occasions as well. Otherwise religiously disaffiliated people will enter the doors of a local church for holidays like Palm Sunday and Easter, Mother's Day, and All Souls Day; cultural celebrations such as the Feast of Our Lady of Guadalupe, Día de los Muertos, or Simbang Gabi; for specific religious ceremonies such as the weddings, baptisms, first communions, confirmations, *quinceañeras*, and funerals for friends or family members, as well as during moments of personal, community, national, or global crises.

Like Lent, these occasions of return are all still very brief. They may last for the duration of a religious ceremony and then, once it is over, the visitors are gone yet again. We have learned from Ash Wednesday, however, that even the shortest moments really do matter. If we acknowledge and respond at these times, a person can be transformed. We are challenged to be mindful of and responsive to the other instances throughout the year. Church leaders can apply the best practices for welcoming Lenten visitors to those who return in these other moments.

Regardless of the circumstances, whether joyous or sad, tragic or momentous, we are bound by our Christian mandate to welcome the stranger, comfort the afflicted, and lovingly encounter the visitor at our door. These are opportunities for every church or congregation to show hospitality and love of neighbor, in the same way that Ash Wednesday is every year.

Beyond Lent, we must always be like Abraham sitting at the entrance of his tent (see Gen 18:1–18), ready to spring into pastoral action at the sight of unexpected guests. Even during the well-planned holiday celebrations and especially on those occasions of unexpected hardship, we really do not know when God will meet us in an encounter during a moment of return. Therefore, we must always be ready and open to the possibilities.

For major holidays like Christmas and Easter, as well as other cultural celebrations that are significant for a particular population, you can apply the principles and suggested ideas laid out in the previous chapters regarding Ash Wednesday and Lent. With Christmas, an added feature is using the secular experiences (like popular holiday movies and music) and helping people make connections to the sacredness of the season. And like Lent, these other seasons and holy days are often associated with childhood, family, nostalgia, and culture, each with their own rich heritage and stories, so be sure to make connections there as well. Some of the other moments of return that we may miss include but are not limited to weddings, baptisms, and funerals. Here are some suggestions for your consideration in addressing those too:

- **Be excited for engaged couples and new parents.** When people come to your church to get married or to have their child baptized, the first reaction—from the person at the front desk to the pastor to anyone who encounters them along the way—should be one of pure joy and excitement. Regardless of any past or present situation, just as on Ash Wednesday or at any other moment of return, church leaders should always make that couple feel completely welcome in the community.

149

- **Instruct greeters to welcome wedding and baptism guests with kindness and joy.** At weddings and baptisms (or at a Sunday service or Mass where a wedding or baptism is taking place), be particularly welcoming to the couple's friends and family who are entering the church for these happy occasions. And while pastors and pastoral leaders may be singularly attentive to the couple getting married or having their child baptized, be sure to be inclusive of their guests too. Make those visitors feel as if the faith leaders are as concerned about them as much as they are focused on the bride, groom, parents, or child. The church might consider offering small gifts or mementos for being present and invite the guests to fill out a welcome/sign-in card. After the ceremony, someone from the church should follow up with a note thanking them for attending and inviting them to join the church community in praying for the newly married couple or the newly baptized child.

- **Encourage the couple to accompany their friends and family.** If a couple is getting married or having their child baptized, there are opportunities to help them grow in their faith and love throughout the preparation for marriage or baptism. However, there is not as much time for the accompaniment of their friends and family who will attend the ceremony. Therefore, encourage the principal couple to accompany their guests along the way. Share ideas with the couple on how best to talk about their faith and how best to support their friends and family with Christian love.

- **Pastorally care for those who return in crisis.** When people reconnect with the Church because of a personal or global crisis moment, it is imperative to be fully present for those individuals. At these fragile moments, they are seeking comfort, support, advice, or a listening ear. One does not need to be a counselor, or the pastor or community leader, to offer pastoral care to a person going through crisis. This idea can also include funerals, homegoings, memorial services, and burial rites.

- **Follow up after the moment of return.** If you gathered contact information for those who return at any of the previously mentioned times, be sure to follow up within two or three days with an email, social media message, phone call, or text (as was recommended after Ash Wednesday). That message should simply be along these lines: "It was great to meet you. I hope the experience was memorable. I am available if you would like to connect again (and adding in any specific details related to your first encounter with them)." Be sure to assess the situation carefully to know whether extending a specific invitation to another event would be prudent in this first outreach. What is most important is getting to know them and, through that, learning and appreciating their story and keeping their intentions and experiences in your prayers.

BEING RESPONSIVE TO PEOPLE'S STORIES

When we take the time to encounter another human being—on Ash Wednesday, during Lent, or at any moment of return—we begin to discover something: everyone has a story, and everyone's story is worth knowing. God gives to each of us a starting point and an end point, giving us life and leading us from this life into eternity. Between those, though, there exists a wonderful, human story that is beautiful. We intrinsically know this because, across time and culture, we love stories—from campfire tales and bestselling novels to theatrical productions and blockbuster movies. Imagine for a moment that every person who makes a moment of return is the protagonist of a long-running television show that has captivated its audience for years. As they walk in the door of our church, the next great episode is about to begin—and we are now the latest guest star in their tantalizing drama. Imagine what that individual's *previously on...* segment would show us and imagine what the *next on...* teaser might reveal. Recognizing the human value of every person and the magnificent story they have for us is a glorious lesson. It can be easy to generalize about strangers in our midst, especially those who may look, think, or act differently from us. It can be tempting for us to presume their backstories and make conclusions based on weak presumptions. But this is not the way of the Christian disciple.

Christ calls us to be better than that. Jesus himself chose to learn the magnificent stories of Matthew and Zacchaeus (Matt 9:9–13 and Luke 19:1–10, respectively) and Simon the Pharisee (Luke 7:36–49) rather than generalize about them. He dined in their homes, walked the roads of Galilee with them, and was enraptured by their realities. In the same way, we are called to appreciate the lived experiences of the people we encounter, no matter the occasion.

Ash Wednesday and Lent give us an opportunity to do this with the yet-unknown guests who arrive at our doorsteps for ashes and the multitudes who join us in our shared Lenten practices. If we truly accompanied people in that penitential season, then we probably were illuminated by the joy of discovery. We recognized the rich depths of another's backstory, the pains they may be carrying, and the origins and depths of their spiritual journey thus far. We rejoiced when we gained a new friend or acquaintance whose story we now better understand. We have been blessed by these Lenten moments, but opportunities to listen to another's story can happen at any time and under any circumstance.

Furthermore, these opportunities are not restricted to religious or spiritual settings. These encounters can take place in our homes and family gatherings. Learning the story of another can occur at the workplace, on the field, or in the classroom. It can happen in our neighborhoods and communities, as well as in online spaces. It can even happen when we keep seeing the same people behind the checkout registers at the grocery store or coffee shop, the same nurses at our local clinic, or the same package delivery carriers at our door. Likely, we have done this already among our networks of friends and families. We learned about and entered their stories. In their imagined television series, we are already part of the recurring cast list, favorite characters integral to the plot. Knowing their origins, realities, and experiences has enriched our relationships with them through the years. Through them, we appreciate the value of story. And once we know another's journey, it can be more difficult to judge them or cast them aside.

It may be helpful to return to the reasons why people often reconnect with churches on Ash Wednesday, originally covered in chapter 2. The seven proposed reasons may not only give us insight for the Lenten season but also reveal how the stories of others can impact our communities throughout the year. We cannot distribute ashes every single week, but we can take inspiration from the motivation that drives people to reconnect for ashes and Lenten traditions.

1. Providing Peace, Rest, and Refuge

The forty-day season reminded us that, at any given moment, most people are dealing with some personal struggle, whether that be living through uncertain transition, experiencing the tragedy of loss or regret, facing alarming financial or health issues, or enduring feelings of pain, insecurity, loneliness, or anxiety, just to name a few. Those struggles often come to the forefront during an introspective season like Lent, and Ash Wednesday may have provided a momentary refuge from the storms, but the deluge continues throughout the year. An increasing number of people are not looking to their local church or religious institution to find a sanctuary for those troubles, sensing that churches offer little or no support for the average and often disaffiliated individual. The very work of pastoral care, however, is one of the sure foundations of the Christian Church since its earliest days, as the author of Acts tells us: "A great number of people would also gather from the towns around Jerusalem, bringing the sick and those tormented by unclean spirits, and they were all cured" (Acts 5:16). The demand for pastoral care was so great that the first apostles developed the diaconate to assist them with the works of charity and service (see Acts 6:1–7). The young Church healed the sick, cast out demons, and provided food and provisions for the poor and the widows in addition to their preaching and teaching ministries.[3]

If this is such a critical component to the Christian story, why don't people perceive churches as places they can find care, concern, or support for their struggles in life? Perhaps we are not doing enough, or if we are, perhaps we are not communicating it to our local communities. If we hope to maintain the engagement of people beyond the Lenten season, we need to take the pastoral direction. Here are some ideas to transform our church buildings into perennial welcoming sanctuaries of peace, rest, and refuge:

- **Notice the quiet ones.** Keep a watchful eye on those who sneak into the back row at our churches, perhaps even a little late to Sunday service or Mass, and who do not interact with others. Be kind to them, for their silence and desire for anonymity may reveal a deeper pain that they are regularly offering up to God. In whatever way possible, without making the situation awkward, offer a gentle word of kindness and support to these individuals on a regular basis.
- **Offer more counseling and spiritual direction.** Provide pastoral counseling, mental health services, and spiritual direction or companionship… and be sure to promote these offerings often in church communications and at Sunday worship. This will ensure visitors and regular churchgoers will know that there are opportunities for support if they need them or if they want to recommend them to others.
- **Increase investment in pastoral care services.** Because of the high numbers of people who are suffering within and beyond our regular church membership, encourage your church to invest more in pastoral care services, mental health resources, and ministries. Some of this may also

mean reorienting existing church efforts toward pastoral care rather than programming and events, especially for younger generations.

- **Strongly communicate your pastoral tone.** *How* we convey our message in Sunday sermons or homilies and in church communications (bulletins, websites, and social media) can be just as important as *what* is conveyed. Tone matters. In the Lenten season, the universal tone across many churches should be one of compassion, acceptance, and inclusion—and therefore many are attracted to the Church during Lent. It is essential to keep projecting that compassionate pastoral tone all year round.

- **Host "sanctuary evenings" at the church.** In a similar manner as the suggestions offered during Lent, hold evenings of peace, rest, and refuge on a regular basis. Allow people to discover sanctuary in your church at any time they need this escape. Communicate these evenings more publicly so that those beyond church membership know this is an option for them in their regular routines. Share with the local area that you are a place that welcomes the stranger, the outcast, and those marginalized by society. Always keep your doors open.

- **Literally welcome refugees.** Even within developed societies, there are many who are fleeing persecution. Migrants are looking for places to feel safe from those who would harm or alienate them. Churches have long been sanctuaries for these types of sojourners. The experience of Lent taught us to be more aware of those on the peripheries. Consider ways that your community may more readily welcome and take care of immigrants and refugees, those who are living in any level of poverty, the person who has been ostracized from their families, or those who are disabled or mobility-challenged, and the deaf community.

2. Highlighting Our Spirituality

The accessibility of Lent's spiritual dimension is an attractive option for those who are seeking a deeper connection to the divine. As noted earlier, in Lent, we often *lead with Jesus* in our pastoral activities during the season literally framed around Jesus's forty-day trek into the Galilean wilderness—and people notice. The spiritual routines of prayer, fasting, and almsgiving are approachable means for guests who want to draw closer to God. The experiences of Lenten reconciliation and the exploration of the life of Christ over the course of six weeks are opportunities for a person to enhance his or her spiritual core and relationship with the Lord. However, at other times of the year, we simply do not talk about Jesus as often as we do in Lent. People also notice this approach, and some avoid further involvement. This shift may fuel the rise of those who consider themselves *spiritual but not religious*, as they do not want to associate with groups that do not emphasize their spiritual core.

When we read Saint Paul's letters in the New Testament, we are reminded of the centrality of God in every missive he pens. To the Galatians, he says, "Paul an apostle—sent neither by human commission nor from human authorities, but through Jesus Christ and God the Father, who raised him from the dead" (Gal 1:1); to the Ephesians, he begins, "Paul, an apostle of Christ Jesus by the will of God, To the saints who are in Ephesus and are faithful in Christ Jesus" (Eph

1:1); and to the Philippians, he writes, "Paul and Timothy, servants of Christ Jesus, To all the saints in Christ Jesus who are in Philippi" (Phil 1:1). No matter his audience and no matter what time of year these epistles were written, Saint Paul always places God up front, and his grounding in Christ informs the spiritual core of his message. We should do this as well. Beyond Lent, what can we do to make our churches not just religious institutions but spiritual havens for all who seek God's graces? Here are some ideas:

- **Provide more spiritual activities and programs.** When planning church programs throughout the year, consider ones that help people grow not only in their religiosity but also in their spirituality. Ensure that there is an obvious spiritual core to all the regular and ecclesial activities that are hosted by your church.
- **Collaborate with religious communities with spiritual charisms.** Emphasize the spirituality of the Church by collaborating with other spiritual and religious groups or organizations in your area. For instance, in the Roman Catholic tradition, there are many consecrated orders of men and women (sisters, brothers, monks, and nuns) that profess a particular *charism* (spirituality or spiritual foundation) such as the Franciscans, Paulists, Jesuits, and Dominicans. Work with these and other groups to infuse a bit of their charism in your local congregation on a more regular basis.
- **Be open to the rich variety of spiritual traditions and experiences.** With its long history and global breadth, Christianity has an incredible diversity of spiritual traditions within itself: contemplative,

advocacy, academic or educational, ecological, eucharistic, devotional, liturgical, mystical, justice-oriented, and many other dimensions. Be aware of this rich variety and provide opportunities to help people connect to any of them, either at your church or somewhere else in the local area.

- **Boldly communicate your focus on Jesus.** In your communications, internally and externally, emphasize the connection to the divine. Although Christ is our core, we cannot underestimate the value of naming it aloud and in print. Boldly share that Christ is the center of all that we do, as well as all the efforts that spring from the community's foundation in Christ: the works for mercy and justice, the call to communal prayer, and the treatment of others, especially those most vulnerable and marginalized.
- **Humbly witness the impact of the gospel in your life.** In addition to church communications, each person in the congregation should grow more comfortable speaking about their personal spirituality in everyday conversations. This will allow them to respond to others' questions and concerns about faith with a positive grounding in spirituality and to share their stories of faith and their perspective on life, all with grace, humility, and patience rooted in the gospel.

3. Affirming Commitment

The relative brevity of a forty-day commitment seems doable for many, even those who are less connected to the institutional practice of the faith. Lent is a perennial opportunity for many to commit to a spiritual discipline and, for a short while, practice challenging or unfamiliar activities. Once the season ends, though, the compulsion to keep a regular practice lessens. Another year passes before a similar commitment is made again.

One could cynically argue that this cycle is a result of a fear of commitment, a construct that many people believe, but one that is based in a mistaken understanding of how most people operate. The opposite is probably more the case. People are increasingly overcommitted and overwhelmed by the number of expectations placed on them by work, personal finances, family responsibilities, the economy, and social obligations.[4] Far from a fear of committing, more individuals are simply managing what they feel they can handle at any one time, and this includes their engagement with religious praxis.

While it may seem laughable to those who are regular churchgoers, the season of Lent does offer people a manageable level of commitment without excessive obligations to an already-stretched populace. But after Easter, are there other practices that might intrigue the busy and committed to continue in a spiritual discipline? Perhaps, but these offerings need to be carefully managed in their communication and presentation.

Furthermore, it is critical that even the smallest commitment be affirmed. Consider the lesson Jesus gives in the Gospels (see Mark 12:41–44) as he observed the temple treasury where many affluent people were donating quite generously. Despite all this giving, he called attention to a poor widow who put in two small copper coins, which were nearly worthless in comparison to the other gifts. He said, "Truly I tell you, this poor widow has put in more than all those who are contributing to the treasury. For all of them have contributed out of their abundance; but she out of her poverty has put in everything she had, all she had to live on" (vv. 43–44).

In the same way, no matter what the occasion during the year, the moderate commitment level that an individual may give should not be compared in relation to the daily or weekly practice of regular churchgoers, but in relation to the person's own life with his or her schedule. Perhaps this person can be made to feel at home in our communities, knowing that their efforts are truly appreciated.

Beyond Lent, what can we do to transform our church into an encouraging environment for people at any level of personal or spiritual commitments? Here are some ideas:

- **Be gentle and patient with those less active in their faith.** Again, tone matters. We do not know the faith journey of others, so we are called to be compassionate and kind, especially with those who have disconnected from religious communities. Our default tone should always be one of gentleness and nonjudgmental understanding.
- **Offer short-term commitments.** Consider providing and communicating more short-term initiatives for people to grow in their spirituality or engage in justice activities throughout the year. These may include commitments of no more than two to four weeks or a certain number of days. Offer short-term projects that respect the full schedules that so many people manage today. Be accepting of those who may take part in only these brief engagements.
- **Affirm all spiritual commitments, no matter their size.** With family or friends, especially those who are less active in religious matters, celebrate and honor their spiritual activities, no matter how brief, limited in scope, or insignificant they may seem to you. Affirm the decision

161

to connect with God in whatever way they connect with the Divine. For the moment, leave it at
that. Do not prod or coerce them beyond their
limits.

- **Invite people to go further.** Over time, positive
reinforcement of limited commitments to spirituality and faith, regardless of their extent, could
spark others' interest in going deeper. When you
notice the time is right, make an invitation to
make slightly longer or more extensive commitments and always encourage those individuals to
continue along the path they are taking.

- **Invest more in ministerial pathways.** To encourage growth in the Christian life, we must create intentional structures and ministries that can
open these pathways. We sometimes complain
about people "graduating" from their faith after
childhood yet may not be investing in or developing ministerial opportunities for furthering
that faith. We must create sustainable transitions
between childhood and adult faith experiences.
This involves making a strong investment in
ministries, especially to youth and young adults,
and in people who organize and support those
looking to grow.

4. Providing Renewal and Resolution

There are several moments throughout the year that serve
as new beginnings. As noted earlier, Ash Wednesday is akin to
New Year's Day, with its focus on resolutions and renewal.
Other starting points in a given calendar year include the first
warm days of spring in northern climates, on Easter Sunday
or Memorial Day (which kicks off the summer season in the

United States), the first days of the traditional academic year in late August or early September, or the Christian new year, liturgically speaking, on the First Sunday of Advent. These occasions are observances that give individuals a chance to start anew.

Most people acknowledge that they fall short and stumble in sinful or imperfect ways. They are fully conscious of their humanity and frailty before God, even if it is difficult to admit or express. Perhaps appreciating the anonymity of the communal experience of Lent, some may feel more comfortable going through the process of personal renewal and resolution alongside others during this special penitential season. However, when this time of introspection concludes, people may lack the means or opportunity to begin this growth journey, even though there are several starting points throughout a given year. Can we replicate the opportunities that Lent brings for renewal and resolution at a time other than Lent? Are there everyday encounters that might lend themselves to making people feel comfortable entering a process of discernment and reflection? The answers should be yes, even if people do not engage their local church in this manner for most of the year. This is something central to the Christian faith, rooted in Jesus's teachings on mercy, forgiveness, and starting anew by the grace of God, who says, "See, I am making all things new" (Rev 21:5). Renewal can take place at any moment in life, and the Church is certainly able to accompany someone through these special times. Beyond Lent, what can we do to provide opportunities within our church communities for second chances and spiritual restoration? Here are some ideas:

- **Be compassionate and merciful.** When we encounter a person in our lives who has messed up or done something wrong, what is our first reaction? Being mindful of our initial response in our personal lives can help us to be more conscious of this on a community-wide level. Our first answer to those who have sinned must emulate Jesus who encountered the woman caught in adultery (see John 8:1–11): with mercy, compassion, and strong defense against those who sit in judgment over another. We are all are frail and broken and have made some regrettable choices in life. Recognizing that Jesus told us, "Do not judge, so that you may not be judged" (Matt 7:1), we can adopt this compassionate spirit all year and with every situation. In your personal encounters and as a community, we can resolve to become less judgmental. Over time, it will be noticed.

- **Develop a year-round mentorship initiative.** Within your church, consider developing a program that trains and equips mentors to share their stories and accompany others. Then, communicate that opportunity to all those in your congregation or parish, including visitors and newcomers who return throughout the year. Connect mentors and those being mentored based on career interests, geography, common faith stories, or hobbies and pastimes, and allow those relationships to grow organically. An excellent guide for grounding this effort is *The Art of Accompaniment* developed by the Catholic Apostolate Center.[5]
- **Better communicate forgiveness and mercy.** Many Christian traditions have different ways to facilitate forgiveness: counseling, spiritual direction, healing services, and the sacrament of reconcili-

ation, among other means. We must better communicate these opportunities for renewal and mercy to those outside our churches. Be mindful of how these opportunities are shared, the way announcements are worded, and the description used in invitations (by using non-jargon-heavy language).

5. Discovering Roots and Identity

On Ash Wednesday, our eyes were opened to a world larger than our own, as we saw ashes on the foreheads of those whom we did not know were Christian and those who may not share our denominational expression. As a Roman Catholic, on Ash Wednesday, I always find wonderful solidarity when my Catholic, Lutheran, Episcopalian, and Methodist friends in the United States and in different countries around the world are all posting on social media about receiving their ashes or starting their Lenten fast. When I walk into stores on that day, seeing fellow customers—complete strangers—with ash on their heads, I sense a certain bond and commonality. For a moment, I feel incredibly united in our shared tradition. This feeling of solidary is also felt on Christmas and Easter, as I observe people dressed in their holiday attire, walking or driving around on those days, realizing we share a common spiritual heritage. But can this feeling of rootedness be experienced in other, less visibly obvious ways during the year?

Pope Francis once told a large crowd of young adults, who gathered for an evening vigil in Panama, "It is impossible for us to grow unless we have strong roots to support us and to keep us firmly grounded. It is easy to drift off, when there is nothing to clutch onto, to hold onto."[6] The grounding we may feel on Ash Wednesday can happen in other moments of life, but it takes a bit more effort than in Lent. At those times, we can help people discover and better appreciate their roots and identities as Christians. It may involve widening our scope and collaborating with other churches on a regular basis. Beyond Lent (or Christmas and Easter, for that matter), we can work together across Christian boundaries to help people discover their roots and their God-given purpose and identity. Here are some ideas:

- **Transform ritual by explaining it.** Host more teaching liturgies or provide explanations when engaged in your tradition's rituals to help those who do not understand them. Even those active in the church may not really grasp their most common rites but may be hesitant to admit it. People, especially those less active in their faith tradition, could be more engaged in these practices if they understood more deeply their meaning and significance. Assume little; explain much.
- **Connect with other Christians in the area.** Be ecumenical and universal by recognizing our interconnectivity. This can start by being more collaborative across Christian boundaries and borders. We share many of the same experiences and we are best when we are united, connected, cooperative, and at peace with one another. Work with your congregation or denomination's ecumenical or interreligious efforts to find out ways to bridge those connections in your community.
- **Recognize and promote a global view of faith.** People are increasingly less parochial and more global. Today, individuals have greater access to news and friends around the world and all with

great immediacy. Ash Wednesday reminds us of the universality of Christian traditions like this, but throughout the year, take a more global view, recognizing that individuals, especially youth and young adults, see a faith community that stretches far beyond your local area. Work with your congregation or denomination to discover what national or international efforts you can tap into.

- **Lower the temperature on social media.** Move beyond infighting among factions and groups in the Church, and work together on a regional, diocesan, ecumenical, area-wide, or global level. It can be tempting to counter fire with fire online but resist this urge. Lent teaches us how connected we all are; however, throughout the year, we can find greater interconnectivity on social media simply by encouraging a culture of civility, respect, and kindness in those environments. Work with your congregation's or denomination's communication leaders and make use of their resources to find creative ways to lower the temperature and bring Christian peace into digital spaces.

6. Encouraging Accomplishment

Bibles and catechisms are not light reading. Their intimidating page count alone is staggering and may visually appear to people as too imposing to attempt. This may also be true of the religious traditions from which they come. When one feels like they are at rock-bottom, when they have failed and floundered, when they have tried but still come up short, the prospect of moving toward religiosity as a next step can be daunting. On Ash Wednesday, a brief breakthrough happens. As we have noted, those who would otherwise avoid religion decide to receive ashes, and during Lent, they commit to a forty-day endeavor. But aside from that, everything else about Christianity might seem beyond their ability—especially if faith seems irrelevant or impersonal.

Look for ways to give people a sense of accomplishment regarding the traditions of the Christian faith. Are there little milestones we can offer that may provide gradual progress in the direction of faith? Lent reminds us that we do not need to make our churches so complex that it takes a degree in theology to fully grasp. We do not need hurdles to be one of the chosen few. Regular participation in Christian devotions or activities, which may seem second nature to churchgoers, can make other people feel like failures. It can drive individuals to avoid us, lest they miss the mark once more. We can make our churches places where individuals can regain self-worth and succeed, during Lent and especially beyond that season. Here are some ideas:

- **Communicate (and follow through on) attainable goals.** When we offer opportunities in our church, clearly state the outcome of the project or program. In some cases, our ambiguity on the purpose of an initiative leaves people with the idea that the goal is unattainable. Communicate well the achievable goals and, then walk with people to help them meet those ends.
- **Simplify the church's processes.** The act of officially becoming part of a community can be quite complicated and convoluted. If simply joining a congregation is difficult, how much more challenging will it be for one to feel at home there? Simplify your registration and membership pro-

cesses, making it easier to be part of your family of faith. Manage the requirements, communicate clearly, streamline the steps, and allow people to accomplish the first task: becoming part of a loving community.

- **Encourage celebration of simple moments of spirituality.** Within your community, should a family member or a friend come to an active churchgoer and say that they find God while walking in nature, encourage them to not dismiss this accomplishment. Promote a culture of celebration for the simple moments and encourage those individuals to share more about their encounter with God. Then suggest that the active churchgoer ask if they could join their friend or family member for the next time they are seeking God (for instance, while walking through nature) so that they, too, can experience what this person has so wonderfully discovered.

- **Affirm all levels of growth, not just the big things.** Look for opportunities to recognize all growth and accomplishment. For instance, when recognizing wedding anniversary celebrations in the community, do not limit your outreach to people who have marked twenty-five or fifty years, but also include those celebrating three or five or ten years of marriage. Within the congregation, consider other overlooked milestones that can be honored, even if they are not commonly accepted as significant occasions. Find ways to affirm personal growth publicly: new jobs, sending a child off to college, birthdays, completing a four-week small group or Bible study, completing a 5K, and so on.

- **Offer genuine gratitude to people who make moments of return.** When parishioners' friends or colleagues mention to them that they went to church for the first time in a long while or did something religious or spiritual within their personal lives, encourage your regular community members to express joy rather than pushing their friends and family for more. Ask them to be positive and thankful for the momentary accomplishments and recommend that they dialogue about these experiences.

7. Helping People Feel They Truly Belong

As noted, people are seeking a sense of belonging. They appreciate that they matter to someone else or that they are not alone. When individuals feel part of a community bigger than themselves, their confidence, self-worth, and faith in others are all boosted. There is a sense of wholeness that can result from the simple feeling of belonging. Rituals like Ash Wednesday and Lenten traditions help to solidify that sense of connection, as those rites bind us to one another. These seemingly routine Christian experiences give us a glimpse into the past, when prior generations engaged in them, and across the world, where so many others are taking part in the same movement. This solidarity enhances belonging.

Community is something that almost every group or institution struggles to maintain. In his advice to business, finance, and social change leaders, Charles H. Vogl, the author of *The Art of Community*, says, "When we see that others are concerned about our own welfare, we'll invest more in building community with them, and we'll feel more connected."[7] In other words, we must invest in people and their lives. We are encouraged to give visitors a sense of belonging, to learn their stories and make them part of ours. This practice should exist no matter the time of year. Transforming our churches into families, where people feel a profound sense of belonging, will encourage individuals to engage more deeply. Here are some ideas:

- **Be more welcoming.** When people walk into your church at any time of year, how are they greeted, or are they greeted at all? From the moment they leave their vehicle or the moment they step foot on church grounds, a visitor should always know that this community wants them to be there. Emulate the father in Jesus's parable of the prodigal son: "While he was still far off, his father saw him and was filled with compassion; he ran and put his arms around him and kissed him" (Luke 15:20). Make a concerted effort to smile and greet individuals with sincere welcome and excitement, even while they are still a far way off.
- **Be mindful of and accompany one another.** We are challenged to look out for each other within our communities. If someone is missing from church one week, do we follow up to see how they are? If a person in our congregation looks downtrodden, do we check in on them, making sure they are alright? Even among newcomers who recently joined your church, follow up and be responsible for their well-being. We should always show care for one another and be attentive to others' needs.
- **Build an outreach for single adults.** Those who are single often feel left out of church communities. Because of the strong emphasis on families in

many parishes and congregations, those who live alone are not always recognized or feel seen by church leaders. Consider developing an outreach ministry for single adults in your area (either of all generations or within a certain age bracket). Be intentional in ensuring that single adults feel engaged, included, and welcomed to help them feel they truly belong.

- **Let people know they are not alone.** All populations, including single, married, and clergy, young and old alike, can develop feelings of loneliness. This is a real issue that is often brushed aside. Lent taught us to help people know they are not alone and to recognize that they have a support system when loneliness creeps into their minds and hearts. Year-round, we should continue to be more aware of the epidemic of loneliness and supporting people with resources for mental health, anxiety, and depression.

- **Be ambassadors of accompaniment.** When Saint Paul says to us on Ash Wednesday, "We are ambassadors for Christ, since God is making his appeal through us" (2 Cor 5:20), that is our signal to reframe every encounter as an opportunity to allow God to touch the heart of another through our words and actions. For every man, woman, and child to feel God's love, in a particular way those who feel isolated and those disconnected from religious institutions, we should see ourselves as one of the conduits of that experience. Through us, God can meet people where they are. We are Christ's ambassadors, helping people know they truly belong to a community where

God can encounter them repeatedly through the kind and loving embrace of one another.

BEING INTENTIONAL CHRISTIANS

By making a concerted effort of entering and connecting another's story to our own journey of faith, we exemplify the fullness of Christian life. Saint Paul summarized from his point of view what it takes to be a good Christian:

> Let love be genuine; hate what is evil, hold fast to what is good; love one another with mutual affection; outdo one another in showing honor. Do not lag in zeal, be ardent in spirit, serve the Lord. Rejoice in hope, be patient in suffering, persevere in prayer. Contribute to the needs of the saints; extend hospitality to strangers.
>
> Bless those who persecute you; bless and do not curse them. Rejoice with those who rejoice, weep with those who weep. Live in harmony with one another; do not be haughty, but associate with the lowly; do not claim to be wiser than you are. Do not repay anyone evil for evil, but take thought for what is noble in the sight of all. If it is possible, so far as it depends on you, live peaceably with all. (Rom 12:9–18)

This passage wonderfully encapsulates those seven year-round lessons we gained through the experience of Ash Wednesday and Lent and extending beyond those moments to the whole year. Through this process, we have learned to provide peace, rest, and refuge ("contribute to the needs of the saints; extend hospitality to strangers...associate with the lowly"), to highlight our spirituality ("do not lag in zeal, be ardent in spirit, serve the Lord"), to affirm others' commitment ("be patient in suffering, persevere in prayer"), to provide renewal and resolution ("Let love be genuine; hate what is evil, hold fast to what is good"), to discover our roots and identity ("live in harmony with one another...live peaceably with all"), to encourage accomplishment ("rejoice with those who rejoice, weep with those who weep"), and to help people feel they truly belong in our communities ("love one another with mutual affection; outdo one another in showing honor"). In some respects, it is not just the newcomers and guests we encounter who are having a moment of return. It is also us.

In these encounters, we are having our own moments of return. At those times, we get to return to the foundation of our faith. In this wonderful passage from his letter to the Romans, Saint Paul invites all of us to return to God and to follow in the footsteps of the one who said, "Come to me, all you that are weary and are carrying heavy burdens, and I will give you rest. Take my yoke upon you, and learn from me; for I am gentle and humble in heart, and you will find rest for your souls. For my yoke is easy, and my burden is light" (Matt 11:28–30). We must return to emulating Christ who welcomed the stranger, healed the broken, offered second chances to the weary, walked with the disciples, and invited all he met to a community where everyone belongs. But there is one more key ingredient that must be done by those who follow the Lord, hinted at in Saint Paul's note at the end of the paragraph. There, he writes, "If it is possible, so far as it depends on you" (Rom 12:18). This conditional clause may seem inconsequential, but it is, in fact, an integral component to our efforts. It is important because, if a congregation really wants to transform itself into a Christian community that projects these values and follows Jesus's lead, it must be intentional about these measures.

Beyond the Ashes

This intentional commitment is critical to anything done for Ash Wednesday and Lent, but it is essential for every other moment of the year. The attraction and natural flow of the Lenten season can be enough to sustain a newcomer or guest through forty days. But as disaffiliation trends have shown us, we cannot rely on chance for a person to retain that connection the other eleven months. We must treat every day like Ash Wednesday: an occasion to actively engage another person, to listen deeply to their story, to encourage them on their journey, and to invite them to walk with you a little further. We must intentionally seek out new and innovative ways to provide dynamic pastoral care; to cheer on and support others' accomplishments, no matter how small they may seem; and to give everyone we meet a sense of belonging. We cannot leave any of this to chance and hope that everything turns out okay.

On every holiday and holy day, at times of celebration and during occasions of mourning, when someone considers returning to a church for a moment or in any potential encounter with a Christian disciple, there should always be considerable and intentional effort on our part to do the very things Saint Paul outlined to the early Christians in Rome and, most important, to emulate the unconditional love of Jesus Christ for all we meet as we look ahead to the future. Being consistently intentional about those seven key strategies for accompaniment and letting ourselves be a part of our visitors' and guests' stories is what can transform our churches into truly becoming a more complete Christian community every single day of the year.

In the past, we may have been unintentional in Lent, at other moments of return, and in our daily encounters with others. We have not always heard or become part of their stories. Because we did not intentionally engage and accompany, these wonderful people have come and gone. *This passivity and reluctance must end now!* When we become more aware of newcomers in our midst, when we take the time to truly listen to others' stories, and when we have a community in which people feel like they belong, then we are surely on the road to transformation. These experiences will certainly remind us we have much still to learn. We will learn from hearing new perspectives, appreciating the others' concerns, and going through a transformative process that allows us to grow, both individually and as a community. All of this, of course, requires humility on our part, acknowledging that, as wise as we think we may be, perhaps we came to an incomplete conclusion or took a wrong direction. This personal journey is itself a transformation, and we can thank Ash Wednesday for opening us up to that year-round.

Chapter 7

PERSEVERING HOPE

Next Year in Jerusalem!

If today you hear his voice, harden not your hearts. (Ps 95:8)

—from the Ash Wednesday Verse before the Gospel

What if this year was a bust? What if we tried but nothing seemed to change? Where do we go next? Or was all of this just a fool's errand? The answer rests in our lasting hope.

f history has shown us anything, it is that perseverance wins the day. Consider the story of Christianity, born in the long shadow of the Roman Empire as early believers hid away in upper rooms and darkened homes under the cover of night. Facing isolation, uncertainty, and persecution, the nascent Church was perseverant to its very core. As Saint Paul said to the Romans, "We also boast in our sufferings, knowing that suffering produces endurance, and endurance produces character, and character produces hope, and hope does not disappoint us" (Rom 5:3–5). The early Christians faced failure, disaffiliation, and setbacks, but they continued their steadfast commitment to God and to one another.

Hope FROM THE Ashes

There is a church in Rome that embodies that spirit. On the summit of the Aventine Hill, there stands an austere house of worship, the Basilica of Santa Sabina, where a Christian community has occupied this land since the second century. The early followers of Christ secretly huddled together in the home of Sabina, a rich Roman widow who was martyred for her faith. Despite the death of their matron and leader, the community endured. They persevered. After centuries of persecution, the Christian faith was legalized by the Roman emperor Constantine in the fourth century. Faced with barbarian invasions several decades later, the community took refuge on the Aventine once more and, in 432, erected a church there in honor of their protectress, Saint Sabina.[1] The basilica has since withstood the test of time. It is truly a symbol of Christian perseverance, not unlike the longevity of ashes and Lent in our history.

Less crowded and busy than the other major hills of the city, the Aventine is located above the noisy fray of the tourists, restaurants, and shopkeepers. This quiet isolation was a reason why the elite Roman senators would make their homes there and Christians would find refuge from persecution and invasion. Without a vehicle, one must cautiously ascend the hill on foot, passing cemeteries and elegant homes. Again, what stands out about this journey is its relative stillness. The climb up the Aventine is not a long walk, which means the vista at its peak can be enjoyed right away. At the highest point on this Roman hill is a simple road connecting Santa Sabina, now the mother church of the Dominican order, and Sant'Anselmo all'Aventino, a Benedictine abbey and college. From an orange grove adjacent to Santa Sabina, a visitor can look northwest over the city of Rome. The dome of Saint Peter's Basilica is visible, as are the colorful rooftops of the cityscape. The smell from the orange trees fills the air and the cool breeze causes the leaves to bristle and flap.

Again, even when groups of tourists scurry about in the near distance, a rich calm can still wash over the astute observer.

Here is where the story of Lent and Santa Sabina come together: Beginning in the fourth century, Christians in Rome gathered with a different community every day of Lent to break their all-day fast. All the pastors, including the bishop of Rome (the pope), celebrated Mass and Vespers with each congregation and, afterward, joined together in a communal meal. Since the sixth century, when Pope Gregory the Great established the official order of these visits, the Ash Wednesday site on this pilgrimage has always been the Basilica of Santa Sabina on the Aventine. The practice faded by the Renaissance but was revived in 1960 by Pope John XXIII.[2] More recently, popes have begun this long-standing tradition by walking the road atop the Aventine's summit from Sant Anselmo to Santa Sabina. Even though these churches have undergone architectural changes over time, one can still sense the deep faith and perseverance of the early Christians who once worshiped there. Santa Sabina's own simple, classic design is a truly fitting place to honor the first day of a season dedicated to Christian simplicity and rootedness.

Stepping into this holy place today, whether on Ash Wednesday or any other day of the year, any visitor can feel the noise and calamity of their world outside suddenly cease, and a future hope, firmly grounded in the past yet also fully aware of the present, begins to emerge. This is the place where countless Christians began their Lenten journeys for many centuries. However, we all cannot travel to this sacred and historical site for the beginning of our annual journeys. Instead, our Lenten season often begins in our local churches, on train platforms and at community centers, in parking lots and schools, or wherever ashes may be distributed. Most of Lent takes place at home, the domestic church, and among friends or family or in private moments of prayer and contemplation.

These spaces should become as sacred and special as Santa Sabina on the Aventine. That *take-your-breath-away* experience in an awe-inspiring ancient basilica must become the norm for every faith community.

Perhaps that did not happen last year. Maybe this was not the experience this past Ash Wednesday or Lent. Perhaps your new initiatives were tried, but the response was not too great. That is okay—because next year is always less than twelve months away and there is no time like the present to begin your preparation.

Perseverance has always been the foundation of Christian faith. Saint Sabina and her brave community of Christians, celebrating their common faith by candlelight in a darkened home on the Aventine, not to mention the centuries of men and women who worshiped here, persevered through violence, plague, famine, war, and uncertainty. Some years were better than others for those early believers. Sometimes things worked and sometimes they made mistakes. But they kept going. If your own church's most recent efforts to be responsive to the Lenten moments of return were not received with glad satisfaction or happy acceptance this year, *keep going*. If your attempt at engaging newcomers and visitors on Ash Wednesday was not a raving success this year, *keep going*. And if your year-round measures to be a more hospitable, attentive community are not proceeding as expected, *keep going*.

Just prior to the Gospel reading on Ash Wednesday, many Christian churches will hear the cantor sing or the reader proclaim this familiar verse from the Book of Psalms: "If today you hear his voice, harden not your hearts" (Ps 95:8). It is tempting to give up and harden our hearts in the face of setback and failure. After working to make things just right for Ash Wednesday or Lent, following all the insights and ideas in this book, leaving the season without those people engaged (or without a flood of new members or parish registrations) can be frustrating. We can harden our hearts, grow cynical, and feel defeated. Instant success probably is not going to happen. After one Ash Wednesday or one Lenten season, engagement of those who are away from church may not notably increase. The hurdles we face are massive: record-breaking disaffiliation of individuals from religious institutions and communities; a crippling surge of personal struggles afflicting people today from racism and poverty to mental health challenges and broken relationships; and limited church and human resources to respond in a comprehensive way to any, if not all, of these concerns. To turn the tide of these realities will not occur after one or two attempts. It will take consistent effort, year after year.

People's confidence in religion or religious groups has been strained after decades of that trust being broken for a variety of reasons. It is not impossible to change that reality, but it does require a reestablishment of that trust. To regain it, the very reason for embarking on this journey must be sincere and without ulterior motives. In other words, the result of this missionary endeavor should not just be an increase in Sunday collections, nor a refilling of the pews, even if that sobering reality may initially spur us to do this work. Rather, to truly gain a person's trust, our motives must be pure and our hearts must not be hardened. We reimagine our approach on Ash Wednesday and Lent and throughout the year because we want to enter into a relationship with other travelers along the road, to give them a sense of belonging, and to share with them the good news that Jesus Christ brings to a weary world.

Grounded in prayer and allowing God to lead us, if we keep this rationale at our core and commit to doing this work every year, trust will begin to form in the hearts of visitors, guests, and newcomers. They will see that we love them, that we want to know their stories, that we wish to learn from them, and that we desire to support them with care and compassion. Perhaps most important, through our loving actions, they will recognize the love that God has for them. This will not happen immediately; it will take time, but "harden not your hearts" because as Saint Paul said, "hope does not disappoint us" (Rom 5:5). Even if they do not suddenly reengage in our churches and communities, we can rest assured that they met Christ in your compassionate outreach, and we discovered Christ alive in them. That encounter fuels our perseverant hope.

In my work in church ministry through the years, I have had plenty of missed opportunities and seen my efforts go seemingly nowhere. I also have witnessed wonderful stories of renewal, refuge, and reconciliation associated with Ash Wednesday and Lent. These stories are part of my inspiration for this book—because I know, with God, all good things are possible, but we must persevere and *keep going*. Several people shared their stories with me as I was writing and researching. Here are a few that I have been permitted to share:

- "Ash Wednesday and Lenten devotions were the first 'Catholic stuff' I did as I moved toward the Catholic Church, even before I felt the call to conversion. It made sense to me in a really deep way" (Amy from Dayton, Ohio).[3]
- "Growing up…Christian churches in my town always did an ecumenical Good Friday Walk. Volunteers would step forward at each stop to help carry a large cross that would lead the procession around town. At each stop…the reflection would connect Jesus's journey and the struggles for equality and social justice.…It was my first experience of publicly demonstrating my faith" (Audrey from Bartlett, Illinois).[4]

- "The first time I ever walked into a church to attend Mass on my own was on Ash Wednesday. That was also the day I came back to the Church" (Caitlyn from Hebron, Indiana).[5]

These wonderful experiences, and countless more, are what give fuel to our fire and hope from the ashes. These stories give us a glimpse into what is possible when we take on an intentional posture of radical hospitality and dynamic accompaniment, when the Holy Spirit is brought together in our moments of genuine encounter. At the end of one of my favorite movies, *Field of Dreams*, Terrance Mann, played by James Earl Jones, makes a statement about baseball that seems strikingly appropriate to our efforts:

It's a part of our past....It reminds us of all that once was good, and it could be again. Oh, people will come....People will most definitely come.[6]

Be patient when things go awry or when an opportunity is missed during a moment of return. The trust being established will not be broken when we fumble, so long as our core mission in Christ is intact. The wondrous thing about an annual occurrence is that it happens every twelve months. As Terrance Mann reminds us, people will most definitely come...again. If this Lent falls short, there is another one less than eleven months away. Ash Wednesday and Lent are resilient in and of themselves. The ashes always have been part of the Christian story and will be part of our story long after we are gone from the earth. Another opportunity will arise next year—and as chapter 6 revealed, the lessons learned can be applied to many other moments throughout the year. Preparations for next Lent can begin at any time—and the sooner those efforts start, the more comprehensive they will be. No matter what day of the year it is right now as you read this, you can begin preparing for the journey to the next Ash Wednesday.

Invite the entirety of the churchgoing community to begin learning about Lent, the potential guests, and the best practices in responding to Lenten visitors with love and compassion. Practice the skills described throughout this book so that you and your fellow leaders are ready when the occasion should come, whether that is on Ash Wednesday or some other critical moment of return. Tell others about your newfound awareness and encourage other active Christians to consider how they are responding to the person who may distrust the Church, get frustrated by Christians, and distance themselves from religious practice for most of the calendar year. Reflect on your own story, your journey of understanding, and what you have learned along the way. Share those insights with loved ones and key leaders in your community. Begin right now.

But whatever you do, do not give up. Because people will most definitely come. Ash Wednesday is like a laboratory for learning the "art of accompaniment" (*Evangelii Gaudium* 169).[7] What we are called to do in Lent is what we are called to do every single day of the year. If we can do this well for forty days, we can do it for forty years or more. Practicing accompaniment in the Lenten season can make us more pastorally responsive, welcoming, ecumenical, evangelizing, loving, compassionate, understanding, and intentional. It can make us more *Christian*. Our communities can be transformed into spiritual havens, places to be trusted, and sanctuaries to refresh the soul for those who are broken and lost. Personal and communal conversion can occur, but it will not happen overnight, perhaps not even after one or two years. We must be patient. We must persevere and hope. We must establish trust. All this will take time and hard work. But remember: "Harden not your hearts."

In the Jewish tradition, at the conclusion of the Seder meal, the domestic commemoration of the Passover of the Lord (see Exod 12:1–28), participants who partake of this meal outside of Israel recite this familiar phrase: *L'shana haba'ah B'Yerushalayim* (‏םילשוריב האבה הנשל‏),[8] which is translated as "Next year in Jerusalem." This sentiment is one of hope and perseverance. The idea is that, despite past setbacks or potential obstacles, each family has a genuine anticipation that next year will be their long-awaited moment of return to the Holy Land. These are the final words of a beloved annual ritual for our Jewish brothers and sisters. As their Seder closes, the recitation of this familiar prayer lingers in the air, puncturing the silence that follows. It seeps into the consciousness of the community. It is a proclamation of hope. In a similar way, we are called to keep persevering and continue striving for pastoral accompaniment every year, because next year might be *the* year when we experience an encounter that could be *the* encounter that moves the heart and soul of our Lenten guests and transforms the moments of return into milestones of faith. Yes, there are times when all seems lost, when our churches and our own lives seem to be covered in sackcloth and ashes. Yet hope, rooted in our faith and the love of God, always perseveres and rises up from those ashes. If you are feeling uncertain about the future, in particular the future of our Christian communities in an age of disaffiliation and deep anxiety, let us look anew at the hope revealed here. Next year in Jerusalem! Anything is possible. May it be so for each of us and all whom we encounter along the way.

Appendix 1

RESOURCES FOR FURTHER EXPLORATION

Armentrout, Don S., and Robert Boak Slocum, eds. *An Episcopal Dictionary of the Church: A User-Friendly Reference for Episcopalians*, s.v. "Ash Wednesday." New York: Church Publishing, 2002.

Bradshaw, Paul F., and Maxwell E. Johnson. *The Origins of Feasts, Fasts, and Seasons in Early Christianity*. Collegeville, MN: Liturgical Press, 2011.

Catholic Apostolate Center. Developed by Colleen Campbell and Thomas Carani. *The Art of Accompaniment: Theological, Spiritual, and Practical Elements of Building a More Relational Church*. Washington, DC: Catholic Apostolate Center, 2019.

DeSiano, Frank P. *The Evangelizing Catholic: A Practical Handbook for Reaching Out*. Mahwah, NJ: Paulist Press, 1998.

The Disney Institute with Theodore Kinni. *Be Our Guest: Perfecting the Art of Customer Service*. Los Angeles: Disney Editions, 2011.

Evangelical Lutheran Church in America (ELCA). "Worship Resources: Frequently Asked Questions; Why and How Do We Use Ashes on Ash Wednesday?" May 2018.

http://download.elca.org/ELCA%20Resource%20
Repository/Why_and_how_do_we_use_ashes_on_Ash
_Wednesday.pdf.

Favazza, Joseph A. *The Order of Penitents: Historical Roots and Pastoral Future*. Collegeville, MN: Liturgical Press, 1988.

Francis, Pope. *Christus Vivit (Christ Is Alive!)*. Washington, DC: USCCB Publishing, 2019.

———. *Evangelii Gaudium (The Joy of the Gospel)*. Washington, DC: USCCB Publishing, 2013.

Greer, James G., Jr. "The Sudden Emergence of the Forty-Day Lent in the Fourth Century." PhD diss., Graduate School of Theology of Nashotah House Seminary, 1972.

Grey, Dr. Mark M. "A Social Scientist's Reflections on Ash Wednesday and Lent." *1964: Nineteen Sixty-Four* (blog). Center for Applied Research in the Apostolate (CARA) at Georgetown University, March 1, 2017. https://nineteensixty-four.blogspot.com/2017/03/a-social-scientists-reflections-on-ash.html.

Grey, Dr. Mark M., and Paul M. Perl. *Sacraments Today: Belief and Practice among U.S. Catholics*. Washington, DC: Center for Applied Research in the Apostolate (CARA) at Georgetown University, April 2008. https://cara.georgetown.edu/sacramentsreport.pdf.

Gueranger, Very Rev. Dom Prosper. "The History of Septuagesima." *The Liturgical Year*. Translated by Rev. Father Shepherd, OSB. The Liturgia Latina Project. Accessed March 10, 2021. http://www.liturgialatina.org/lityear/.

Gulevich, Tanya, and Mary Ann Stravros-Lenning (illustrator). *Encyclopedia of Easter, Carnival, and Lent*. Detroit: Ominigraphics, Inc., 2002.

Jarzembowski, Paul. "Mobilizing the Field Hospital: Pastoral Care as a Paradigm for Ministry with Young Adults." *Religions* 11 (November 19, 2020): 617. https://doi.org/10.3390/rel11110617.

Jastrow, Morris, Jr. "Dust, Earth, and Ashes as Symbols of Meaning among the Ancient Hebrews." *Journal of the American Oriental Society* 20 (1899): 133–50.

Jastrow, Morris, Jr. et al. *Jewish Encyclopedia.com: The Unedited Full-Text of the 1906 Jewish Encyclopedia,* s.v. "Ashes." New York: Funk & Wagnalls Company, 1906. https://jewishencyclopedia.com/articles/1944-ashes.

Lynch, Peter. *The Church's Story: A History of Pastoral Care and Vision.* Boston: Pauline Books and Media, 2005.

Martin, Donald Jay. "Ash Wednesday in Tudor England: A Study of Liturgical Revision in Context." PhD diss., University of Notre Dame Theology Department, 1978.

Meeks, Blair Gilmer. *Season of Ash and Fire: Prayers and Liturgies for Lent and Easter.* Nashville: Abingdon Press, 2003.

Nocent, Adrien. *The Liturgical Year: Lent, the Sacred Paschal Triduum, Easter Time.* Vol. 2, Translated by Matthew J. O'Connell. Collegeville, MN: Liturgical Press, 2014.

Rivers, Robert S. *From Maintenance to Mission: Evangelization and Revitalization of the Parish.* Mahwah, NJ: Paulist Press, 2005.

Russo, Nicholas V. "The Early History of Lent." Waco, TX: The Center for Christian Ethics at Baylor University, 2013. https://www.baylor.edu/content/services/document.php/193181.pdf.

Springtide Research Institute (Josh Packard, Executive Director). *Belonging: Reconnecting America's Loneliest Generation.* Bloomington, MN: Springtide Research Institute, 2020.

Talley, Thomas J. *The Origins of the Liturgical Year.* New York: Pueblo Publishing Company, 1986.

Tanner, Norman. "A Short History of Lent." *Thinking Faith* (blog). March 15, 2011. Accessed January 30, 2021. https://www.thinkingfaith.org/articles/20110315_1.htm.

Hope FROM THE Ashes

United Methodist Church, Section on Worship of the Board of Discipleship. *From Ashes to Fire: Services of Worship for the Seasons of Lent and Easter with Introduction and Commentary.* Nashville: Abingdon Press, 1979.

United States Conference of Catholic Bishops, Committee on Divine Worship. "What Is Lent?" Accessed March 10, 2021. https://www.usccb.org/prayer-worship/liturgical -year/lent.

United States Conference of Catholic Bishops, Committee on Evangelization and Catechesis. *Living as Missionary Disciples: A Resource for Evangelization.* Washington, DC: USCCB Publishing, 2017.

Vogl, Charles H. *The Art of Community: Seven Principles for Belonging.* Oakland, CA: Berrett-Koehler Publishers, 2016.

Appendix 2

ASH WEDNESDAY READINGS

As I shared in the preface and as you have noticed throughout this book, the Ash Wednesday readings guided our journey. In so doing, we discovered "hope from the ashes." The Scriptures used by many churches on this day tell a rich biblical story that we can claim as our own. We can put ourselves in the community the prophet Joel urges to return with haste or the one the apostle Paul encourages to go out as ambassadors for Christ. We can join the Psalmist's song of repentance and sit at Jesus's feet as he gives us the tools for gospel living in his Sermon on the Mount. Having these scriptural passages at hand throughout the year can prepare and equip us to be missionary disciples eager to welcome the stranger, give comfort to those who struggle, and walk with any individual we will encounter along our shared path toward and with the Lord.

Please note that the following readings are those common to several Christian traditions; however, there are notes for times when other Scriptures are used (or extended). Consult directly with your church to confirm the exact readings you may be using for Ash Wednesday within your faith community.

Hope FROM THE Ashes

First Reading
Joel 2:12–18

Even now, says the LORD,
    return to me with your whole heart,
    with fasting, and weeping, and mourning;
Rend your hearts, not your garments,
    and return to the LORD, your God.
For gracious and merciful is he,
    slow to anger, rich in kindness,
    and relenting in punishment.
Perhaps he will again relent
    and leave behind him a blessing,
Offerings and libations
    for the LORD, your God.

Blow the trumpet in Zion!
    proclaim a fast,
    call an assembly;
Gather the people,
    notify the congregation;
Assemble the elders,
    gather the children
    and the infants at the breast;
Let the bridegroom quit his room
    and the bride her chamber.
Between the porch and the altar
    let the priests, the ministers of the LORD, weep,
And say, "Spare, O LORD, your people,
    and make not your heritage a reproach,
    with the nations ruling over them!

Why should they say among the peoples,
'Where is their God?'"

Then the LORD was stirred to concern for his land
and took pity on his people.

NOTE: Some Christian communities add Joel 2:1–2 to the above text; other communities use Isaiah 58:1–12 instead for the Old Testament reading.

Psalm Response
Psalm 51:3–4, 5–6ab, 12–13, 14, 17

R. Be merciful, O Lord, for we have sinned.

Have mercy on me, O God, in your goodness;
in the greatness of your compassion wipe out
my offense.
Thoroughly wash me from my guilt
and of my sin cleanse me.

R. Be merciful, O Lord, for we have sinned.

For I acknowledge my offense,
and my sin is before me always:
"Against you only have I sinned,
and done what is evil in your sight."

R. Be merciful, O Lord, for we have sinned.

A clean heart create for me, O God,
and a steadfast spirit renew within me.

Hope FROM THE Ashes

Cast me not out from your presence,
and your Holy Spirit take not from me.

R. Be merciful, O Lord, for we have sinned.

Give me back the joy of your salvation,
and a willing spirit sustain in me.
O Lord, open my lips,
and my mouth shall proclaim your praise.

R. Be merciful, O Lord, for we have sinned.

NOTE: Some Christian communities use Psalm 103:8–14 for the responsorial reading.

Second Reading
2 Corinthians 5:20—6:2

Brothers and sisters:
We are ambassadors for Christ,
as if God were appealing through us.
We implore you on behalf of Christ,
be reconciled to God.
For our sake he made him to be sin who did not
    know sin,
so that we might become the righteousness of
    God in him.

Working together, then,
we appeal to you not to receive the grace of God
    in vain.
For he says:

*In an acceptable time I heard you,
    and on the day of salvation I helped you.*

Appendix 2

Behold, now is a very acceptable time;
behold, now is the day of salvation.

NOTE: Some Christian communities add 2 Corinthians 6:3–10 to
the epistle reading.

Verse Before the Gospel
See Psalm 95:8

If today you hear his voice,
harden not your hearts.

Gospel Reading
Matthew 6:1–6, 16–18

Jesus said to his disciples:
"Take care not to perform righteous deeds
in order that people may see them;
otherwise, you will have no recompense from
  your heavenly Father.
When you give alms,
do not blow a trumpet before you,
as the hypocrites do in the synagogues and in
  the streets
to win the praise of others.
Amen, I say to you,
they have received their reward.
But when you give alms,
do not let your left hand know what your right
  is doing,
so that your almsgiving may be secret.
And your Father who sees in secret will repay you.

"When you pray,
do not be like the hypocrites,

who love to stand and pray in the synagogues and
    on street corners
so that others may see them.
Amen, I say to you,
they have received their reward.
But when you pray, go to your inner room,
close the door, and pray to your Father in secret.
And your Father who sees in secret will
    repay you.

"When you fast,
do not look gloomy like the hypocrites.
They neglect their appearance,
so that they may appear to others to be fasting.
Amen, I say to you, they have received
    their reward.
But when you fast,
anoint your head and wash your face,
so that you may not appear to be fasting,
except to your Father who is hidden.
And your Father who sees what is hidden will
    repay you."

NOTE: Some Christian communities add Matthew 6:19–21 to the
Gospel reading.

NOTES

CHAPTER 1

1. Jeffrey M. Jones, "U.S. Church Membership Falls Below Majority for First Time," *Gallup*, March 29, 2021, https://news.gallup.com/poll/341963/church-membership -falls-below-majority-first-time.aspx.

2. Mark M. Grey, "Sacraments Today Updated," *1964: Nineteen Sixty-Four* (blog), Center for Applied Research in the Apostolate (CARA) at Georgetown University, August 16, 2016, http://nineteensixty-four.blogspot.com/2016/08/sacraments-today-updated.html.

3. Grey, "Sacraments Today Updated."

4. Patricia Jarzembowski (office manager, St. Joseph Catholic Church, Dyer, IN), email message to author, February 2, 2021.

5. Mark M. Grey and Paul M. Perl, *Sacraments Today: Belief and Practice among U.S. Catholics* (Washington, DC: CARA at Georgetown University, April 2008), 86, https://cara.georgetown.edu/sacramentsreport.pdf.

6. Grey and Perl, *Sacraments Today*, 86.

7. Ælfric, *Lives of Saints: A Set of Sermons on Saints' Days Formerly Observed by the English Church*, trans. Rev. Walter W. Skeat (London: Early English Text Society by N. Trübner & Co., 1881), 262–66.

8. Morris Jastrow Jr., "Dust, Earth, and Ashes as Symbols of Mourning among the Ancient Hebrews," *Journal of the American Oriental Society* 20 (1899): 144.

9. Homer, *The Iliad*, trans. Alexander Pope (online version retrieved via "The Project Gutenberg EBook of *The Iliad of Homer* by Homer," Sept. 2006), book 18, 546, https://www.gutenberg.org/files/6130/old/6130-pdf.pdf.

10. Joseph A. Favazza, *The Order of Penitents: Historical Roots and Pastoral Future* (Collegeville, MN: Liturgical Press, 1988), 251–52.

11. Tertullian, *Treaties on Penance: On Penitence and On Purity*, trans. William P. Le Saint, SJ, STD (Westminster, MD: Newman Press, 1959), 31–32.

12. Paul F. Bradshaw and Maxwell E. Johnson, *The Origins of Feasts, Fasts, and Seasons in Early Christianity* (Collegeville, MN: Liturgical Press, 2011), 89–113.

13. James G. Greer Jr., *The Sudden Emergence of the Forty-Day Lent in the Fourth Century* (Nashotah, WI: Graduate School of Theology of Nashotah House Seminary, 1972), 1.

14. Dr. Richard P. Bucher, "The History and Meaning of Ash Wednesday," Our Redeemer Lutheran Church, Lexington, KY (blog), accessed March 8, 2021, https://web.archive.org/web/20140413044542/http://www.orlutheran.com/html/ash.html.

15. Herbert Thurston, "Ash Wednesday," *The Catholic Encyclopedia*, vol. 1 (New York: Robert Appleton Company, 1907), http://www.newadvent.org/cathen/01775b.htm.

16. Tanya Gulevich and Mary Ann Stravros-Lenning (illustrator), *Encyclopedia of Easter, Carnival, and Lent* (Detroit: Ominigraphics, 2002), 52.

17. Mark M. Grey, "The End of 2020," *1964: Nineteen Sixty-Four* (blog), December 30, 2020, http://nineteensixty-four.blogspot.com/2020/12/the-end-of-2020.html.

18. According to Dr. Mark Grey (Director of CARA Catholic Polls and Senior Research Associate at CARA), approximately 19 percent of all self-identified U.S. Catholics (which

amounts to 72.4 million people, according to CARA's *Frequently Requested Church Statistics* at https://cara.georgetown .edu/frequently-requested-church-statistics/) went to Ash Wednesday services in person in 2021, matching the numbers who attended in person for Christmas 2020. He notes, "Those two days were the highest physical attendance since the pandemic [in 2020–21] began." Mark M. Grey, email message to the author, March 1, 2021.

19. The Vatican Congregation for Divine Worship and the Discipline of the Sacraments published a "note" on the imposition of ashes for February 2021 for the COVID-19 pandemic, asking those distributing ashes to sprinkle them over the top of each person's head rather than mark the forehead, the normal custom in several nations including the United States. Vatican News, "Vatican Modifies Distribution of Ashes for Ash Wednesday," Vatican News Service, January 21, 2021, https://www.vaticannews.va/en/vatican-city/news/ 2021-01/ash-wednesday-coronavirus-note-distribution-ashes .html.

20. Donald Jay Martin, *Ash Wednesday in Tudor England: A Study of Liturgical Revision in Context* (PhD diss., University of Notre Dame Theology Department, 1978), 74.

21. Nicholas Pocock, *Troubles Connected with the Prayer Book* (Westminster: Camden Society New Series, 1884), vol. 38, p. 165, art. 7.

22. United Methodist Church, Section on Worship of the Board of Discipleship, *From Ashes to Fire: Services of Worship for the Seasons of Lent and Easter with Introduction and Commentary* (Nashville: Abingdon, 1979), 14.

23. Google survey response from John (from Sauk Village, IL), January 1, 2021, and an email message to the author, February 5, 2021. NOTE: This and most of the survey responses (and email conversations) that follow in this book were submitted with an understanding that full names of the interviewees would be withheld. If last names are used, there was a mutual agreement for such an identification.

24. Blair Gilmer Meeks, *Season of Ash and Fire: Prayers and Liturgies for Lent and Easter* (Nashville: Abingdon Press, 2003), 107–8.

25. Rev. Heidi Haverkamp, email messages to the author, February 4 and 10, 2021.

26. Pastor Peggy Marks, interview with the author, February 10, 2021.

27. Eugeniusz Klimakin, "Why Do Poles Have Ash Sprinkled on Their Heads?," *Culture.pl*, February 28, 2017, https://culture.pl/en/article/why-do-poles-have-ash-sprinkled-on-their-heads.

28. Joyce Zako, email message to the author, February 9, 2021.

29. Gerard Gallagher, email message to the author, January 19, 2021.

30. Jack Beresford, "Record Number of Catholics Attend Drive-Thru Ash Wednesday Service in Ireland," *The Irish Post*, March 7, 2019, https://www.irishpost.com/news/record-number-catholics-attend-drive-thru-ash-wednesday-services-ireland-165060.

31. Gallagher, January 19, 2021.

32. Louisa Wright, "Lent Survey: More Than Half of Germans Think Fasting 'Makes Sense,'" *DW News*, February 18, 2018, https://www.dw.com/en/lent-survey-more-than-half-of-germans-think-fasting-makes-sense/a-42549446.

33. "Lent 2017: 59 Percent Want to Do Without," *The-Health Site.Com: Scientific-Practical Medical Journal*, accessed February 11, 2021, https://en.the-health-site.com/lent-59-percent-want-to-do-without-5323.

34. Wright, "Lent Survey."

CHAPTER 2

1. "What's With the Ash?," interview by the editors of Busted Halo Ministries, with music by Kevin MacLeod, March 9, 2011, https://www.youtube.com/watch?v=Xmpa00ekOE0.

2. Google survey response from Heather (from Roslyn, PA), January 18, 2021.

3. Google survey response from Tim (from Valparaiso, IN), January 15, 2021.

4. Google survey response from Becky Eldredge (from Baton Rouge, LA), January 4, 2021.

5. Dan Kimball, *They Like Jesus but Not the Church: Insights from Emerging Generations* (Grand Rapids, MI: Zondervan, 2007), 34.

6. Google survey response from Allison (from Palatine, IL), January 21, 2021.

7. Google survey response from Jennifer (from Malta), January 19, 2021.

8. Google survey response from Chris (from Liverpool, UK), December 30, 2020.

9. Google survey response from Deanna (from Arlington, VA), January 15, 2021.

10. Google survey response from Alexis (from Wheaton, IL), January 15, 2021.

11. Google survey response from Barbara (from Mokena, IL), January 18, 2021.

12. Google survey response from Diana Hancharenko (Saint Angela Merici Parish, Youngstown, OH), January 4, 2021.

13. Leonel L. Mitchell, *The Meaning of Ritual* (Harrisburg, PA: Morehouse Publishing, 1977), 114.

14. Google survey response from Jacki (from Chicago, IL), January 22, 2021.

15. Google survey response from Nino (from Aldie, VA), January 5, 2021.

16. Google survey response from Cathleen (from Perkasie, PA), January 19, 2021.

17. This experience is described in more detail by author Admiral William H. McRaven (U.S. Navy Retired), *Make Your Bed: Little Things that Can Change Your Life...and Maybe the World* (New York: Grand Central/Hachette, 2017).

18. Google survey response from Fr. Greg Friedman, OMF (from Albuquerque, NM), January 25, 2021.

19. Arthur C. Brooks, "Go Ahead and Fail: Perfectionism Can Make You Miserable; Here's How You Can Muster the Courage to Mess Up," *The Atlantic*, February 25, 2021, https://www.theatlantic.com/family/archive/2021/02/how-overcome-fear-failure/618130/.

20. Google survey response from Corrine (from Lockport, IL), January 1, 2021.

21. Dr. Mark M. Grey, "A Social Scientist's Reflections on Ash Wednesday and Lent," *1964: Nineteen Sixty-Four* (blog), Center for Applied Research in the Apostolate (CARA) at Georgetown University, March 1, 2017, https://nineteensixty-four.blogspot.com/2017/03/a-social-scientists-reflections-on-ash.html.

22. Grey, "A Social Scientist's Reflections."

23. Springtide Research Institute (Josh Packard, Executive Director), *Belonging: Reconnecting America's Loneliest Generation* (Bloomington, MN: Springtide Research Institute, 2020), 71.

24. Google survey response from Claudia (from Arlington, VA), January 5, 2021.

25. Google survey response from Bill (from Lowell, IN), January 16, 2021.

26. Facebook direct message to the author, February 17, 2021.

27. Pope Francis, *Christus Vivit* (*Christ Is Alive!*) (Washington, DC: USCCB Publishing, 2019).

28. Pope Francis, *Fratelli Tutti* (*On Fraternity and Social Friendship*) (Washington, DC: USCCB Publishing, 2020).

29. Pope Benedict, *Deus Caritas Est* (*God Is Love*) (Washington, DC: USCCB Publishing, 2006).

30. Archbishop Desmond Tutu, "Desmond Tutu on Compassion," interview by Marc Ian Barasch, *Psychology Today*, March 1, 2005, last reviewed June 9, 2016, https://www.psychologytoday.com/intl/articles/200503/desmond-tutu-compassion.

31. Pope Francis, *Evangelii Gaudium* (*The Joy of the Gospel*) (Washington, DC: USCCB Publishing, 2013).

CHAPTER 3

1. Mark M. Grey, "Sacraments Today Updated," *1964: Nineteen Sixty-Four* (blog), Center for Applied Research in the Apostolate (CARA) at Georgetown University, August 16, 2016, https://nineteensixty-four.blogspot.com/2016/08/sacraments-today-updated.html.

2. United States Conference of Catholic Bishops, Committee on Evangelization and Catechesis, *Living as Missionary Disciples: A Resource for Evangelization* (Washington, DC: USCCB Publishing, 2017), 9.

3. The "way of proceeding" for the *National Dialogue on Catholic Pastoral Ministry with Youth and Young Adults* can be found online in their *Final Report* (Washington, DC: NFCYM, 2021) at https://formationreimagined.org/wp-content/uploads/2021/03/NDreportEN.pdf.

CHAPTER 4

1. Google survey response from James Behan (associate director for young adult ministry and marriage and family life, Archdiocese of New Orleans), January 22, 2021.

2. John Grosso (digital media director, Catholic Diocese of Bridgeport, CT), email message to the author, February 2, 2021.

3. Fr. Rafael Capo (vice president, Saint Thomas University, Miami), email message to the author, February 1, 2021.

4. Matt Kresich, "Today Was a 'Different' Ash Wednesday. I Present a List of My Random Thoughts throughout the Day," Facebook, February 17, 2021, https://www.facebook.com/matt.kresich/posts/4928453027225484.

5. "Ashes to Go: Taking Church to the Streets," accessed January 31, 2021, https://ashestogo.org/.

6. Rev. Heidi Haverkamp (Episcopal priest and author), email message to the author, February 10, 2021.

7. *The Rule of Benedict*, 53.1–2. Taken from "Chapter 53: The Reception of Guests," commentary by Philip Lawrence, OSB, Monastery of Christ in the Desert, Abiquiu, NM, accessed February 1, 2021, https://christdesert.org/prayer/rule-of-st-benedict/chapter-53-the-reception-of-guests/.

8. The Disney Institute, with Theodore Kinni, *Be Our Guest: Perfecting the Art of Customer Service* (Los Angeles: Disney Editions, 2011), 4, 28–29, 68–69.

9. Google survey response from Nicole Perone (national coordinator, ESTEEM, Milford, CT), January 4, 2021.

10. Google survey response from Kelly (from Washington, DC), December 30, 2020.

11. Google survey response from Katie (from Munster, IN), January 15, 2021.

12. Adrien Nocent, *The Liturgical Year: Lent, the Sacred Paschal Triduum, Easter Time*, vol. 2, trans. Matthew J. O'Connell, introduced, emended, annotated by Paul Turner (Collegeville, MN: Liturgical Press, 2014), 24.

CHAPTER 5

1. Greek translation from *The Precise Parallel New Testament*, ed. John R. Kohlenberger III (New York: Oxford University Press, 1995), 974.

2. Pope Francis, *Christus Vivit* (*Christ Is Alive!*) (Washington, DC: USCCB Publishing, 2019).

3. See https://www.pemdc.org/programs/new-movers-mailing-list/new-movers-program/ for details.

4. For a starting point, consider the insights of the young adults who gathered in Rome in 2018 for a "pre-synodal meeting" with the Vatican and shared their wisdom about mentorship in its *Final Document* (specifically in section 10): http://www.synod.va/content/synod2018/en/news/final-document-from-the-pre-synodal-meeting.html.

5. The term *meat* in association with Catholic fasting is often connected to "flesh meat," or any meat from warm-blooded birds or mammals with skin, as opposed to cold-blooded animals such as fish (or reptiles or amphibians).

6. *Code of Canon Law* §1253, accessed February 21, 2021, http://www.vatican.va/archive/cod-iuris-canonici/eng/documents/cic_lib4-cann1244-1253_en.html.

7. The *Pastoral Statement on Penance and Abstinence* issued by the National Conference of Catholic Bishops (NCCB) in November 1966 encourages "works of voluntary self-denial and personal penance which we especially commend to our people for the future observance of Friday, even though we hereby terminate the traditional law of abstinence binding under pain of sin." Catholics are still asked to make every Friday a day of "penitential observance," which can include abstinence from eating meat on those days; however, the dietary obligation now only pertains to Lenten Fridays. *Pastoral Statement on Penance and Abstinence* excerpted from *Pastoral Letters of the United States Catholic Bishops* Washington, DC: United States Catholic Conference, Inc., 1983), https://www.usccb.org/prayer-and-worship/liturgical-year-and-calendar/lent/us-bishops-pastoral-statement-on-penance-and-abstinence.

8. Mark M. Grey and Paul M. Perl, *Sacraments Today: Belief and Practice among U.S. Catholics* (Washington, DC: Center for Applied Research in the Apostolate [CARA] at Georgetown University, April 2008), 84, https://cara.georgetown.edu/sacramentsreport.pdf.

9. Paul Clark, "No Fish Story: Sandwich Saved His McDonald's," *The Cincinnati Enquirer*, February 20, 2007. Reposted in *USA Today* online, accessed February 21, 2021, https://usatoday30.usatoday.com/money/industries/food/2007-02-20-fish2-usat_x.htm.

10. Deb Debczak, "Why the Filet-O-Fish Sandwich Has Been on the McDonald's Menu for Nearly 60 Years," *Mental Floss*, February 18, 2019, https://www.mentalfloss.com/

article/573930/why-mcdonalds-filet-o-fish-sandwich-was
-invented.

11. Michael P. Foley, *Why Do Catholics Eat Fish on Friday? The Catholic Origin to Just About Everything* (New York: Palgrave Macmillan, 2005), 119.

12. Grey and Perl, *Sacraments Today*, 86.

13. Google survey response from Katie (from Indianapolis, IN), January 15, 2021.

14. In his book, *Googling God: The Religious Landscape of People in Their 20s and 30s* (Mahwah, NJ: Paulist Press, 2007), author and national Catholic leader Mike Hayes shares (pp. 27–30) that one of the key reasons why those in their twenties and thirties do not come to church is because their busy lives have *eclipsed* a connection with faith.

15. National Dialogue on Catholic Pastoral Ministry with Youth and Young Adults, *National Dialogue Final Report* (Washington, DC: National Federation for Catholic Youth Ministry, 2021), 82.

16. Fifteenth Ordinary General Assembly of the Synod of Bishops, *Final Document of the Synod of Bishops on Young People, Faith and Vocational Discernment* (Vatican City: Libreria Editrice Vaticana, 2018), §46.

17. AmeriCorps, "Volunteering and Civic Life in America: National—Age Group Rates," Corporation for National and Community Service, April 16, 2019, https://data.americorps.gov/Volunteering-and-Civic-Engagement/National-Age-Group-Rates/fgxe-8vu3.

18. "Charitable Giving Statistics," National Philanthropic Trust: 2020, accessed February 24, 2021, https://www.nptrust.org/philanthropic-resources/charitable-giving-statistics/.

19. Google survey response from Anna (from Seattle, WA), February 21, 2021.

20. The United States Conference of Catholic Bishops (USCCB) provides some helpful guidelines for Christians engaging with the Jewish community or Jewish traditions, including the Passover Seder/Haggadah. See https://www

.usccb.org/prayer-and-worship/liturgical-year/lent/questions -answers-catholic-jewish-relations.

CHAPTER 6

1. Pope Francis, *Evangelii Gaudium* (*The Joy of the Gospel*) (Washington, DC: USCCB Publishing, 2013).

2. Pope Francis, *Christus Vivit* (*Christ Is Alive!*) (Washington, DC: USCCB Publishing, 2019), http://www.synod .va/content/synod2018/en/fede-discernimento-vocazione/ -christus-vivit---post-synodal-exhortation-to-young-people -and-t.html.

3. With his experiences as a priest, pastoral theologian, author, and grief counselor, Peter Lynch wrote a compelling narrative of the primacy of pastoral ministry and its ongoing development in Christian history in his book *The Church's Story: A History of Pastoral Care and Vision* (Boston: Pauline Books and Media, 2005). In it he reminds the reader that pastoral accompaniment is integral to the work of the Church.

4. A study by the American Psychological Association (APA) notes, "Survey findings illustrate a scenario in which Americans consistently experience stress at levels higher than what they think is healthy" and that commitments and expectations around money (69 percent), work (65 percent), the economy (61 percent), and family responsibilities (57 percent) are the top contributors to this trend (*Stress in America™: Missing the Health Care Connection* [Washington, DC: American Psychological Association, February 2013], 13). The full report can be found here: https://www.apa.org/ news/press/releases/stress/2012/full-report.pdf.

5. See https://www.catholicapostolatecenter.org/art-of -accompaniment.html (accessed September 3, 2021).

6. Pope Francis, "Address at the Vigil, XXXIV World Youth Day in Panama (January 26, 2019)," *L'Osservatore Romano*, January 28–29, 2019, §6, http://www.vatican.va/ content/francesco/en/speeches/2019/january/documents/ papa-francesco_20190126_panama-veglia-giovani.html.

7. Charles H. Vogl, *The Art of Community: Seven Principles for Belonging* (Oakland, CA: Berrett-Koehler Publishers, 2016), 9.

CHAPTER 7

1. Hilary J. Carpenter, *A Short Guide to Santa Sabina* (Rome: Ufficio Libri Liturgici, 1962), 9, 12.

2. Carpenter, *A Short Guide*, 15–16.

3. Google survey response from Amy (from Dayton, OH), January 18, 2021.

4. Google survey response from Audrey (from Bartlett, IL), January 16, 2021.

5. Google survey response from Caitlyn (from Hebron, IN), January 15, 2021.

6. "Scene 29: People Will Come," *Field of Dreams*, written and directed by Phil Alden Robinson (1989; Universal City, CA: Universal Pictures Home Entertainment, 2004), DVD.

7. Pope Francis, *Evangelii Gaudium* (*The Joy of the Gospel*) (Washington, DC: USCCB Publishing, 2013).

8. Rabbi Alfred J. Kolatch, *The Concise Family Seder* (Middle Village, NY: Jonathan David Publishers, 1987), 48.